GOD IN A BROTHEL

An Undercover Journey into
Sex Trafficking and Rescue

Daniel Walker

IVP Books

An imprint of InterVarsity Press
Downers Grove, Illinois

InterVarsity Press
P.O. Box 1400, Downers Grove, IL 60515-1426
World Wide Web: www.ivpress.com
E-mail: email@ivpress.com

InterVarsity Press® is the book-publishing division of InterVarsity Christian Fellowship/USA®, a
movement of students and faculty active on campus at hundreds of universities, colleges and schools
of nursing in the United States of America, and a member movement of the International Fellowship
of Evangelical Students. For information about local and regional activities, write Public Relations
Dept., InterVarsity Christian Fellowship/USA, 6400 Schroeder Rd., P.O. Box 7895, Madison, WI
53707-7895, or visit the IVCF website at <www.intervarsity.org>.

All Scripture quotations, unless otherwise indicated, are taken from the Holy Bible, New
International Version®. NIV®. Copyright ©1973, 1978, 1984 by International Bible Society. Used
by permission of Zondervan Publishing House. All rights reserved.

While all stories in this book are true, some names and identifying information in this book have
been changed to protect the privacy of the individuals involved.

For legal and security reasons, the name of the author has also been changed. "Daniel Walker" is
his pseudonym.

Cover design: Cindy Kiple
Interior design: Beth Hagenberg
Images: set of wings: ©hermi/iStockphoto
        girl sleeping: ©Kamil Vojnar/Trevillion Images

ISBN 978-0-8308-3806-6

Printed in the United States of America ∞

Library of Congress Cataloging-in-Publication Data

Walker, Daniel, 1967-
  God in a brothel: an undercover journey into sex trafficking and
rescue / Daniel Walker.
        p. cm.
  Includes bibliographical references.
  ISBN 978-0-8308-3806-6 (pbk.: alk. paper)
  1. Human trafficking—Prevention—Case studies. 2. Sex-oriented
businesses—Case studies. I. Title.
  HQ281.W34 2011
  261.8'3315092—dc22
  [B]
                                                           2011013669

P 18 17 16 15 14 13 12 11 10 9 8 7 6 5 4 3 2 1
Y 26 25 24 23 22 21 20 19 18 17 16 15 14 13 12 11

For my parents

Contents

Preface

I was hungry and you gave me something to eat,
I was thirsty and you gave me something to drink.

Matthew 25:35

I was imprisoned in a brothel and you rescued me.

This is the story of my infiltration into the multibillion-dollar global sex industry and the human slavery that supports it. It is an exciting story of danger and dramatic rescue. It is a tragic story of horrific exploitation, criminal abuse and gut-wrenching despair. It is the humbling story of a man who set out to follow God but ended up on the pathway to hell.

For the sake of all of those women and children who remain imprisoned and enslaved inside brothels all over the world, I hope this book will challenge and motivate others to bring them rescue and freedom.

While combating human trafficking I worked for three different organizations, one as an employee and two on a contractual basis. It was an honor to serve with each of them and to work alongside the dedicated and passionate people who make up their ranks. Each agency had its own strengths and weaknesses, some of which become apparent in my story.

It is not my intention to criticize, blame or in any way hinder their life-saving and life-changing efforts. Indeed in some cases the methods used by a particular group have since been changed, and some of the people I refer to no longer work for the organizations concerned. To ensure that none of the agencies discussed in this book are identifiable, city names, with the exception of those in the continental United States, have been fictionalized. Deployment locations have been generalized to larger geographical areas. Case histories and other related details have been changed.

I was and am completely responsible for all of the choices and actions I took during my time in this industry. I freely chose to participate in this work, and I chose to remain in the fight when things were not going as planned.

As a police officer I have approached this book with a desire to be as factual as possible while preserving the dignity and safeguarding the identities of the many victims and undercover investigators involved. The names and personal details of those contained in this book have therefore also been altered to protect the individual involved.

As a follower of Christ, serving Jesus is central to my motivation and passion for this work. Nevertheless I am aware that not everyone who reads the following pages will share my allegiance. So I have written in a manner I hope is accessible to everyone.

As a New Zealander I have endeavored to write with humility, well aware that New Zealand is a small nation with a relatively short history. Other countries, due to their geography, history, population growth and cultural diversity, have had to face challenges that we have never had to address.

Finally, as a husband, I write with the knowledge that this story would not have been possible without the unwavering trust and faithful devotion of my wife, Alice. The currency I used to purchase the time of every prostituted child and victim of sex trafficking was her faithfulness and sacrificial love. Every story contained within the following pages is a testament to her belief that every child deserves to be safe from abuse and free from exploitation.

1

South Asia

Her Name Is Daya

The slums of Munpur are a sprawling rabbit warren of tin shacks and dirt pathways, gaping sewers, decomposing garbage, oppressive odors and cramped living conditions. And this is just for the lucky ones. Those with no home sleep on the sidewalks, under concrete overpasses and on the narrow median strips in the roads and highways. Entire families huddle together under plastic and cardboard; children and newborn babies sleep only inches away from speeding vehicles and their acrid fumes.

In one such slum community on the northeast side of Munpur, a girl runs a brothel. She runs it because she is the only occupant. The brothel is a small concrete dwelling with a tin roof. The building has a concrete floor and a sturdy wooden door but is otherwise no different from the many thousands of small dwellings that surround it. It has no address, no name, no amenities and no advertising. The furniture inside consists of one bed.

It is a thriving business nonetheless, and each day a man comes to collect the daily take and delivers food and water to the girl. The only other visitors the girl has are the stream of customers who pass in and out of her bed at all times of the day and night, paying her less than one U.S. dollar for the use of her small body.

And small it is, because the girl is only twelve years old.

I had been deployed to Munpur to assist some of my colleagues
in securing the cooperation of the police to rescue a number of
victims of human trafficking and forced prostitution. This concrete shack was to be our first target. After several days of negotiation, the police commander had finally agreed to assist. Standing
in the hot sun outside the police station, I went over our plan one
last time.

Coordinating a raid on such a target is fraught with difficulty.
First, there is no immediate way to distinguish the building from
the many that surround it, and locating a place that has no obvious landmarks nearby is problematic. Second, like most shanty-
towns and slums of the developing world, the small city has its
own word-of-mouth communication system. Whenever a police
vehicle or other stranger enters its environs, word spreads faster
than fire, doors are bolted, and those operating on the fringes of
the black market disappear. Third, such a community has its own
understanding of dispensing and enforcing justice. Forcing our
way into the heart of their neighborhood raises real safety issues
for a raiding party, especially if one of those entering is Caucasian,
standing out against the sea of dark faces. Last, when certain police officers from the local substation are known to be corrupt and
in partnership with those making money from the abuse of children, asking them to assist in the rescue of the girl is effectively
asking them to cut their own financial throat.

Nevertheless, in the company of a team of local police officers
we believed were honest, we finally entered the slum and made
our way as fast as we could in our rented four-wheel-drive vehicles
to the target.

SLUMDOG RAID

Arriving outside the building, it became apparent that we had
caught the locals off-guard. The degree to which the community

was involved in illegal activity of one kind or another was evident when the police stepped from the vehicles. Men, women and children of all ages began running from every doorway, scurrying down alleyways and disposing of all manner of illicit items as they went. We were, however, only interested in one concrete building and in one small, red, wooden doorway.

Standing in the now-deserted dirt pathway, the police sergeant began knocking on the door. "Open up! Police!" he barked. Other staff had already been positioned at the rear of the building. Standing just to the side of the door, I strained to hear any response or movement from inside. We held our breath to see whether the girl was still there. When there was no response to the pounding and the yelling, I asked, "Can I have a go at kicking the door in?" The sergeant's mustache twitched as he considered my suggestion. Without answering he continued to pound on the door, "Open up!"

At last there was an audible click from inside and the small door swung open.

As we stepped into the darkness from the bright sunshine, the slim form of a young girl slowly came into focus. Standing barefoot beside her bed she wore a dirty white cotton dress. Her straight black hair was pulled back in a ponytail from her face. She was beautiful, with striking eyes and a clear complexion. She was alone. She was confused. She was scared.

Leading her from the darkness of her tiny hovel into the bright sunlight, safety and freedom, I felt overwhelmed by a sense of gratitude, joy and protectiveness. Gratitude that everything had so far gone according to plan and that the girl had been found. Joy that she would now be cared for and that I had the honor of participating in her rescue. As if she were my own little sister, I walked beside her, affording her the protection of a bodyguard, my vigilant yet cold stare communicating to anyone watching that I would ruthlessly defend my small charge.

After placing her inside one of the police vehicles, the female social workers on our team quietly communicated to her that she was not in any trouble but rather that she was forever liberated from the brothel and from her work there. The girl's demeanor slowly changed and her shoulders eased. Most profoundly, a small but stunning smile broke across her face, and she began communicating in her native tongue.

As the small police convoy began to make its way out of the slum city, the girl suddenly pointed to a man in the distance who had been watching the whole affair with great interest. In an animated fashion the girl began conversing with the police officers and the social workers. By the time I received the translation, the man was vanishing into the crowd. Leaping from the vehicle with one of the police officers, I began to chase the man responsible for her imprisonment and her daily exploitation.

Sprinting into an even smaller network of alleyways reminiscent of an Indiana Jones movie set, I pushed my way past pungent food stalls, drying clothes, stray dogs and playing children. Running through the smoke of burning garbage and leaping over open sewers, I was determined not to lose my quarry. However as I came to an intersection in the alleyway I found that we had lost sight of our man and had no idea which path he had taken.

A small crowd began to materialize around me, fascinated to see a white man in their own tiny part of the world. And on the fringes of the crowd it was then that I first saw an increasing number of defensive faces, eyes burning with anger. As frustrated as I was to be so close to the perpetrator and knowing the police would do little more to locate him after we left, discretion seemed the better part of valor. We quietly withdrew to the safety of our vehicles and drove out of the area.

Back at the police station the local commander sat on one side of the interrogation table and the girl, Daya, sat on the other. Her wide eyes and small form were protected on either side by two female social workers, holding her hands, encouraging her and reassuring her. Standing behind them, they reminded me of two angels sitting quietly beside their ward, communicating by their presence all Daya needed to know.

GRATITUDE AND TRANSFORMATION

Without thinking I quietly began to sing under my breath one of the worship songs I had learned in my youth. It was one of those rare moments when my heart spontaneously began thanking God for who he is: Father to the fatherless and defender of vulnerable orphans. I thanked him too for allowing me to experience the sheer exhilaration and joy of having a part to play in the dramatic transformation of a young life. I knew that her life and my life would never be the same again.

Standing in the heat of the summer within the confines of a small police courtyard on the outskirts of Munpur, I realized I was praising God not just for who he is and for what he had done in history, but crucially for what he had done through me that very day.

I began to wonder what would happen if men everywhere embraced their God-given destiny to defend and protect the vulnerable women and children in their communities. What would happen if, in addition to unleashing their strength, skills and passion on the sports field, in the office or behind their computer screens, they discovered their true masculinity by answering this call to arms and to action.

I wondered what would happen if the church worldwide took the offensive against oppression and slavery so that such acts of rescue and restoration occurred every day? What would happen within our faith communities if we became proactive in the face of such injustice? Indeed how would our own families, our own discipleship be forever changed if we were all actively involved in some way in rescuing the oppressed and defending the orphan, advocating for the widow.

I also began to wonder what would happen if churches all over the world mobilized their congregations to proactively take the light of Christ into the dark places of sexual slavery in their own communities and cities. What could possibly affect his church more profoundly and influence the world more significantly than meeting God within the darkness and depravity of a brothel.

FACTS: *Sex Trafficking*

- Sex trafficking is the largest form of modern-day slavery in the world today and is a massive global industry earning organized criminal networks billions of dollars annually.

- Sex trafficking is the recruitment and transportation of a person for the purpose of commercial sexual exploitation and profit. Unlike human smuggling, which involves a contractual relationship between those seeking to travel and those acting as their smugglers, trafficking is a business that preys on the vulnerable using force, fraud, deception, coercion and abduction. Only the trafficker gains out of such a transaction.

- Victims are often abducted or lured by traffickers posing as job recruiters, smugglers or marriage brokers. Sometimes the traffickers are relatives, friends or an intended spouse. When the victims arrive at their destination, their passports and documents are typically confiscated and they are forced to work under threat of rape, physical violence, starvation and deportation.

- More than two million children are exploited in the worldwide commercial sex industry. Trafficking in children often involves exploitation of the parents' extreme poverty. Parents may sell children to traffickers to pay off debts or gain income, or they may be deceived by promises of a better life for their children. In many countries, trafficked children have often lost one or both parents to the AIDS crisis.

- The people who endure the worst forms of commercial sexual abuse throughout the world are typically poor women and children. They are abused, exploited and locked into sexual slavery simply because they can be. They are the world's most vulnerable people.

- This "rape for profit" industry would not exist without the demand for commercial sex flourishing around the world.

2

Superhero

It's not who I am underneath. It's what I do that defines me.

Batman Begins

I always wanted to be a superhero. Not with tights and a cape but the kind of hero every boy aspires to be.

Growing up, I worshiped Zorro, the Lone Ranger and the Bionic Man. I read every Commando comic, watched every war movie and closely followed the adventures of every modern-day savior, be they Luke Skywalker or James Bond. I would regularly lose myself for hours playing war games with friends, imagining my heroic part in all the great battles of history.

As I grew older I began to look forward to fulfilling my own destiny in some modern-day struggle of good versus evil. The only two vocational options attractive to me were those of a soldier or a police officer. I determined to give my heart and soul to one or the other.

In high school I did everything possible to prepare myself for the role I would one day assume. I played those sports I believed would ultimately assist me in my quest, such as shooting, karate and athletics. I chose my friends carefully, studied hard and assumed leadership roles within the school. By the time I graduated, I had ensured I possessed the necessary skills to be the perfect candidate.

My initial applications went well. I passed all the required examinations and interviews and believed I was well on my way to fulfilling my dreams. When I received letters from both the New Zealand Army and the New Zealand Police explaining that my poor eyesight disqualified me from ever serving in either role, I was devastated.

GIRLS AND GRACE

Like many young people in search of meaning and a purpose worthy of them, I enrolled at university. I welcomed the opportunity to explore the great ideas, theories and economies that have shaped human history and development. Having attended a boys-only school, I also enjoyed being surrounded by so many attractive young women. When one particularly engaging young woman invited me to accompany her to hear a visiting Christian speaker, I quickly agreed. Frankly, I would have agreed to go anywhere with her!

Growing up as a child I had attended Sunday school at a local Anglican church in our neighborhood, but I had long since discarded faith traditions as boring and largely irrelevant to modern life. Despite this, I was intrigued by the very reasonable and intellectually sound argument presented in support of the deity of Christ. Ultimately, however, even though what the visitor said made sense, my heart was unconvinced.

Several months later, I was with some friends in the center of my city when we began flirting with a group of young women. We ended up following them into the town hall only to find ourselves at a Youth for Christ concert. Slowly, over the course of the evening, my attention shifted from the girls we were pursuing to some of what the speaker, John Pritchard of Youth For Christ New Zealand, was saying.

As he talked about a God of "amazing grace," I remember thinking that it was all very nice—this God who was good and who apparently liked me. I was, however, looking for something more.

Then the speaker said something that was to change my life forever. One short sentence cut through all my questions and all my doubts. One sentence reached out to me through the crowd and grabbed my heart: "The love and grace of God is a free gift, and there is nothing you can do to earn it. But it will cost you everything."

The spirit inside me that hungered for adventure leapt at this fantastic invitation and amazing challenge. I decided there and then that I could spend the rest of my life searching the world over and never find a greater purpose or a nobler mission.

I believed I had finally found the heroic opportunity I had been dreaming of all my life, and a destiny that would demand my all. So I got up out of my seat and went forward that night, adding my name to the book of life. I made a choice and set off down a path from which there was no return. I embraced the challenge and agreed to persevere through whatever lay ahead.

THE KINGDOM OF GOD

I devoured all of the books and literature I could get my hands on about this mission of love. I joined a church and enjoyed the companionship of others following the same call and living by the same code.

During my second year at university I had the opportunity to attend a three-day conference where American sociologist Tony Campolo was speaking. He was to have a profound influence on my thinking and my life. For the first time I learned that the Christian faith is not primarily focused on the elimination of personal sin. Campolo explained that what God was especially passionate about was seeing his kingdom of righteousness and justice established on earth. Thanks to Tony I also saw that while God loves all people the same, because he is just, he necessarily sides with those who are impoverished and oppressed.

We see this theme throughout the Old Testament: "The victim commits himself to you; / you are the helper of the fatherless" (Psalm 10:14), and "The LORD works righteousness / and justice for the oppressed" (Psalm 103:6). And it continues in the teaching of Jesus:

> The Spirit of the Lord is on me,
>> because he has anointed me
>> to preach good news to the poor.
> He has sent me to proclaim freedom for the prisoners
>> and recovery of sight for the blind,
> to release the oppressed. (Luke 4:18)

I discovered that God hates injustice, and that the harshest words in the Bible are reserved for those who exploit the innocent and the vulnerable: "he was appalled that there was no one to intervene" (Isaiah 59:16).

Again, in the words of Jesus: "I was hungry and you gave me nothing to eat, I was thirsty and you gave me nothing to drink. . . . I tell you the truth, whatever you did not do for one of the least of these, you did not do for me" (Mathew 25:42, 45).

Like all of my childhood heroes, I was amazed to learn that God was a warrior who was quick to rescue those who cried out to him for freedom. I loved the way God sidestepped the religious and the self-righteous, but made himself fully available to those who were humbly willing to acknowledge their humanity. I was inspired by psalms such as:

> You hear, O LORD, the desire of the afflicted;
>> you encourage them, and you listen to their cry,
> defending the fatherless and the oppressed,
>> in order that man, who is of the earth,
>> may terrify no more. (Psalm 10:17-18)

Even more amazing to me was the way that God so profoundly identified with those at the bottom of society. I embraced the mystery inherent in the biblical teaching that when I gave to the poor, I was actually giving to God, as in Proverbs 19:17 (TNIV): "Those who are kind to the poor lend to the Lord." And "'He defended the cause of the poor and needy. . . . Is that not what it means to know me?' declares the Lord" (Jeremiah 22:16).

During my third year at university I volunteered as an area representative for the World Vision 40 Hour Famine. Many schools in New Zealand take part in this annual fundraising event, but it was the first time university students had been targeted and encouraged to participate. The focus of the famine that year was children living on the streets and in rubbish dumps of the developing world. As the local representative I was responsible for accurately communicating the goals of the famine with the university community, and I therefore carefully read and digested all of the information sent to me.

As a child I had read *Oliver Twist*, the Charles Dickens classic tale of child abuse and exploitation. Given my middle-class upbringing in New Zealand, I assumed that such things no longer occurred. Yet my bubble was burst by the stories I read, and I was horrified to learn of the millions of children forced to fend for themselves, and in many cases sell themselves just to survive. Like the founder of World Vision, I asked God to "break my heart with the things that broke his heart." True to his word, God was quick to oblige.

And as I grew to love this God who was both Creator and heroic Rescuer, I wanted to know him more, not just about him. I wanted to know God in the same way that I knew my friends: intimately, emotionally, painfully, genuinely and authentically. I wanted to understand this mystery of grace that could not be controlled, manufactured, manipulated, contrived or demanded. And so I determined to follow him to the darkest places on earth and to look for him in the eyes of all those held captive there by suffering and evil.

After finishing my bachelor's degree, I obtained a scholarship that allowed me to travel to Philadelphia in the United States. I spent two years completing a master's degree in third world development, under the guidance and leadership of Tony Campolo, Ronald Sider and other Christian activists. The master's program was established to train young people to more effectively use their education and skills to transform impoverished communities around the world, empowering those most in need to help themselves.

The focus of my study during this time was on street children, particularly those forced into prostitution. I studied the causes and the solutions, as well as the myriad ways in which others had brought positive change through community development projects. Determined to put my newfound knowledge into practice, I returned to New Zealand and began applying for jobs within the development sector.

Unfortunately, at the time many relief and development organizations were trying to employ fewer expats and more indigenous staff. In keeping with the best practices, they had determined that qualified locals who knew the language, culture and customs would be far more likely to succeed in their efforts, and they would also be a lot less expensive to employ than a foreigner. As my job applications were declined, my frustration and impatience grew.

Having tried to follow the dream I believed God had given me only to end up unemployed was disconcerting to say the least. I had not lost my childhood ambition of becoming a police officer and so I began to reexplore that option. I figured that if God was not going to open the doors for me to achieve his goals, then I would just go and pursue my own.

Prior to 1992, New Zealand had a separate law enforcement

agency tasked with policing traffic law. The Traffic Safety Service (TSS) also had different entry requirements than the police, including a lower eyesight standard. Several months after my return from the United States, I learned that a merger between the police and the TSS was likely. I therefore applied to join the TSS and successfully completed the recruit course. I was thrilled when only eight months later, the merger went ahead and I became a sworn police officer.

MARRIAGE

Not long after joining the police, I was pursued by a college sweetheart. Alice was beautiful, passionate, genuine and kind.

We shared the same faith as well as the same desire to see children rescued from abuse. On the same day that Alice asked me to marry her, I received in the mail a book titled *The Mystery of Marriage* by Mike Mason. A masterpiece of writing, it was the first time I had felt truly challenged by the demands of committed love required by marriage. Indeed, it was the first time I considered marriage as a wild frontier, promising more wonder and adventure than anything else on earth.

For me, getting married had never been high on the list of objectives, and it necessarily entailed letting go of many of the dreams and ambitions I had carried since childhood. I wrote, and then read at our wedding ceremony, the following paraphrase from 1 Corinthians 13:

> If I speak with the charm and sophistication of James Bond 007, but have not love, I am only a resounding gong or a clanging symbol.
>
> If I have the gift of being faster than a speeding bullet, stronger than a locomotive and am able to leap tall buildings in a single bound, but have not love, I am nothing.
>
> If I live in Sherwood Forest and together with my merry

men steal from the rich and give to the poor, and even die in the process, but have not love, I gain nothing.

A real hero, as I have learned, is patient and kind. A real hero does not envy or boast, and is not proud. A real hero is never rude or self-seeking and keeps no record of wrongs. A real hero does not delight in evil but rejoices with the truth. A real hero always protects, always trusts, always hopes, always perseveres.

If a real hero loves—he or she will never fail. The bionics of the Six Million Dollar Man will one day cease. The sword of Zorro will one day be stilled. The white stallion of the Lone Ranger will pass away.

When I was a child I thought like a child, I talked like a child, I reasoned like a child. When I became a man I put childish ways behind me.

For the real heroes among us, these three remain: faith, hope and love. But the greatest of these is love.

This day and everyday, with the help of God, I pray that I will always be a real hero.

RESCUE THE OPPRESSED

After working for several years in the criminal investigation branch of the police, a close friend directed me to an organization based in New York. The group used the skills of criminal investigators from around the world to rescue victims of injustice and oppression. This included documenting the murder and abuse of street children and the prostitution of children.

For me it seemed like a match made in heaven and a role God had been preparing me for all my life. I was very excited at the prospect of utilizing my life experience, education and law-enforcement training on behalf of those who had no one else to turn to. After finding out more about the organization and the individuals behind it, I duly applied for a full-time position.

Knowing that the work required us to relocate to the United States and for me to be away from home for more than 50 percent of the time, Alice had real reservations. We talked, prayed and sought counsel from friends and elders within our church. While not denying the importance of the nuclear family, they reassured us that God also called his people to serve the wider human family with sacrificial love and costly discipleship.

In 2002 we sold our house and moved to America. Despite Alice's misgivings, I was excited to have the opportunity to fulfill my lifelong goals and dreams. I had little idea at the time that following this path would ultimately lead me to working undercover in more than a dozen countries, infiltrating organized criminal groups involved in a modern form of human slavery known as sex trafficking.

I would not have believed that I would soon be traveling alone to exotic and dangerous destinations equipped with James Bond–style gadgets and equipment. I could never have foreseen the role I would have in facilitating the rescue of hundreds of women and children from the very worst forms of sexual exploitation.

With all my idealistic naivety I could also never have imagined the tremendous cost this work would have on me personally. Had I known the unimaginable pain I would one day experience, I would have given up then and there. Indeed, had I glimpsed just a little of the suffering I would witness and the heartbreak I would endure, I would have fled in the other direction. And if I had just an inkling of the grief and distress that Alice would experience as a result of my decision, I would have kept running and never looked back.

But I could not foresee any of these things. And so I embarked on a journey into some of the darkest places on earth: to the bars and brothels of the developing world and to the strip joints and gentlemen's clubs of the global elite. I looked for God in the eyes of the women and children imprisoned there. I found suffering beyond imagination, tears, grief and trauma beyond understanding. And many years later, with tears in my eyes, I remembered my decision to follow this God no matter what the cost.

3

Latin America

Her Name Is Maria

Pressing her small body into mine, she grabbed my hands and placed them on her backside, encouraging me to pull her closer as we swayed and moved across the dance floor. With a different client, these attempts at seduction may have worked. However, the girl looking into my eyes was all of sixteen years old, and her makeup and forced smile failed to conceal her fear, her youth or her genuine desperation.

It was late at night and I was in one of about twenty small brothels that lined both sides of a dead-end street in the worst part of Tolima City. This southern-most city of one of the poorest countries in the world is a major transit point for young girls fleeing the poverty and violence of Central and South America. Many of them are brought here by force, having been sold to the "coyotes," or human traffickers, who operate with impunity in this very corrupt and largely indifferent part of the world.

Maria was no exception. At the age of eleven or twelve she had been casually raped and discarded by a group of men in her local neighborhood in one of the many squalid barrios of Honduras. Maria became pregnant as a result, and after she had her baby she was, like any mother, desperate to find a way to support her child.

Leaving her precious newborn with her own mother, Maria journeyed north in the hope of finding work. Like many hundreds of thousands of girls just like her, what she found instead was a small army of ruthless men and corrupt government officials only too willing to use her vulnerability for their own financial advantage.

Sold to the brothel by a group of traffickers who had ensnared her at the border, Maria was told she now had to pay off her purchase price or debt before she could be free. With threats of further rape and beatings hanging over her head, Maria did her best to sell her small body to the many locals, tourists and miscreants who found their way onto her dance floor.

She had tried to run away and had been taken across into Honduras by the local authorities only too eager to deport the many illegal immigrants who violate their southern borders. She was then picked up by the very same coyotes who had profited from her once before.

Now, with twice the debt to repay and the gang rapes and beatings still fresh in her memory, Maria knew better than to try to escape again. She also knew better than to trust any of her captors or her customers, many of whom were local policemen who received free "services" for their complicit cooperation and "protection" of the industry.

So it was that I found myself looking into the eyes of a child, a mother, desperate to provide for her own baby and desperate to survive another night in hell. Taking my hands in her own and placing them lower still on her backside, she wanted to make sure there was no doubt in my mind that she was mine to consume anytime I wanted her.

I had already captured the brothel owner on the covert camera I was wearing, receiving payment for the purchase of Maria's sexual services. I was confident that, with my testimony, I possessed sufficient evidence under local law to successfully prosecute the owner and facilitate the rescue of Maria and the many other young girls who were being held in captivity there.

Having paid for her sexual services as part of the evidence gathering process, the difficulty I now faced was extracting myself from the situation without arousing the suspicion of the management or otherwise offending or further endangering Maria. Maria was also very reluctant to let me go, as I represented her only potential source of income for the evening. In a moment of rare inspiration and with quiet desperation, I closed my eyes and began to pray.

And then, quite suddenly, everything changed.

FEAR AND EPIPHANY

I had not been conducting investigations into sex trafficking for very long, and being inside a brothel still left me feeling vulnerable and afraid. I was afraid of my own sinful nature. I was afraid of the perpetrators and corrupt officials who were profiting from the organized crime. And I was afraid of going into what I perceived to be enemy territory.

As I prayed, I felt as if a veil had lifted and I saw for the first time a child greatly loved by God, in whose life evil had been allowed to flourish and triumph. And in that instant I was filled with hate and anger. Hatred for the evil that had left her so thoroughly enslaved and devoured, and anger at an indifferent world that so easily allowed its children to be violated, systematically abused and exploited.

A still, small voice reminded me that, "greater is he that is in you, than he that is in the world" (1 John 4:4 KJV). I was reminded that I had in my possession a secret weapon in the form of the truth, carefully documented and saved on my undercover camera. In that knowledge I realized that if anyone was dangerous in that brothel, it was me! Those using Maria to satisfy their lust and for their profit were the ones who needed to fear, because the evidence I had gathered could send them to jail for a very long time.

Fear of my own capacity to sin was gently replaced with a courage and a confidence that was not my own.

The words of an old hymn I had sung during my own childhood then came to mind; "This Is My Father's World." Again I saw for the first time that the brothel I was standing in was as much a part of God's creation as any beautiful mountain or crystal cathedral, and that God had in no way surrendered it to anyone.

I knew that God was in that brothel before I arrived, suffering with Maria, witnessing her defilement night after night and sharing in her tears, and that he would remain in the brothel long after I left. Any uncertainty I previously had about walking into such a dark and "evil" place vanished.

Though not in an audible sense, I nevertheless heard his command and his call to go boldly in his name to such places as these, to rescue the oppressed, defend the orphan and to plead for the widow.

Having made an excuse as to why I had to leave without having sex with her, Maria walked me to the doorway of the brothel. Taking my hands in her own and looking me in the eye, she asked if I was coming back for her. I had not communicated anything of my real purpose for being there. But perhaps, at some deeper level where words cease and communication begins, she sensed that I was different from her typical customers.

Looking her in the eye, I smiled casually and told her that I would be back soon. Having learned to read men's eyes, Maria sensed my uncertainty. Accepting it as she had accepted every other deception in her life, she began to sing me a song in her native tongue. Burying my frustration and powerlessness at having to leave her behind, I gave her a hug and departed.

I subsequently conducted numerous operations throughout the developing world. I had the opportunity to participate in many successful operations that resulted in the rescue of many hundreds of women and children from slavery and international sex trafficking. I gave evidence at numerous trials around the world that resulted in the successful prosecution and conviction of many perpetrators. And as a result of our work, many women and children were placed in safe and secure aftercare facilities where they could receive the care and restoration they needed.

Along with the successes also came the failures. Corrupt authorities, inadequate aftercare facilities, organized crime and human pride led to many failures. For a number of reasons, despite my best efforts and the efforts of the human rights organization I was working for, I was unable to return to the brothels of Tolima City.

A proposed operation to facilitate her rescue was subsequently aborted and Maria, like so many others, is still waiting for someone to invade her darkness.

FACTS: *Corruption*

- There are a host of international declarations and conventions that relate to the suppression of forced prostitution, trafficking and sexual slavery. In addition most countries already have adequate laws to deal with sex trafficking and sexual slavery. The problem is usually therefore not inadequate laws but the enforcement and implementation of those laws. In *Sex Slaves*, Louise Brown writes, "The law has less to do with the reality of the sex industry and far more to do with political considerations and the image a society wishes to project of itself. The law is usually an irrelevance for the sex industry."

- The global commercial sexual exploitation of women and children continues to flourish and expand, in large part due to the corruption of those police, politicians and bureaucrats charged with their protection. For example, of the attempted police interventions and attempted rescues conducted by a human rights organization in south Asia, many failed due to some kind of interference or corruption, typically in the form of a tipoff by the police.

- In many countries the police themselves are doing or facilitating the trafficking, participating as clients and receiving bribes and protection money. Some even own the brothels. In many developing countries the police are not well paid, and the money received from brothels constitutes a significant part of their income.

- For the majority of girls imprisoned illegally in brothels around the world, their only hope of rescue from a system that is rife with corruption is an honest police officer or the intervention of an outside organization.

4

Critics

*It is not the critic who counts. Not the man who points out
where the strong man stumbled or where the doer of great
deeds could have done them better. The credit belongs to those
who are actually in the arena, who strive valiantly; who know
the great enthusiasms, the great devotions, and spend themselves
in a worthy cause; who at best, know the triumph of high
achievement; and who, at the worst, if they fail, fail while daring greatly, so
that their place shall never be with those cold and
timid souls who know neither victory nor defeat.*

Theodore Roosevelt

I loved the casework model our work was based on. In other words, rather than try to combat "human trafficking" or "the prostitution of children" as global issues in and of themselves, the organization addressed one case at a time. Rather than advocating at a national or international level for the elimination of such exploitation, we would document, intervene and then advocate on behalf of one victim at a time.

We knew that by rescuing one victim and successfully prosecuting one offender, we were bringing about change in the community and culture and ultimately the country within which we worked. And slowly, almost imperceptibly, by doing so we were effectively addressing the global issues that surrounded them.

I was, however, amazed to discover that there were many critics of our work. The reasons for their opposition were as many and varied as there were opponents.

LEGALIZATION OF PROSTITUTION

Those pushing for the decriminalization of prostitution were perhaps some of our most vocal critics. Some within their ranks saw our desire to rescue people from prostitution as antithetical to their own efforts to normalize, destigmatize and legalize the sex industry. Once it was explained that our focus was only on those who were victims of forced or coerced prostitution (or children whose age meant they legally could not consent to such activity), we were usually able to sidestep this emotive minefield by focusing on what we all agreed was illegal and worthy of intervention.

That being said, from my experience inside bars and brothels around the world, and from meeting the many hundreds of prostitutes who worked there, I would be doing them a gross disservice to pretend that there are not degrees of freedom and more subtle forms of exploitation involved in every case. What broke my heart on many occasions was hearing the stories of women who were equally enslaved by poverty, sexism, gender inequality or addiction. While they fell outside the narrow legal definition of "forced" or "trafficked" and were therefore beyond our ability to assist, they longed for an alternative means of survival and for the opportunity to escape the invisible chains that held them.

In the fight against sex trafficking, it is important to come together and work in cooperation with those on all sides of the debate and from both ends of the political spectrum. Many of those advocating for the rights of women to prostitute themselves do so out of genuine concern and compassion for those within the commercial sex industry. However, from what I have seen firsthand, I believe they are misguided. The literature about the harms of prostitution is also crushingly conclusive—prostitution hurts those used as sexual commodities. Those who disagree with me and who want to normalize the commercial sex industry should honestly consider how they would feel if their own daughter, granddaughter, younger sister or niece chose a "voluntary" life as a prostitute.

One of the other arguments used to denigrate the work of intervention and rescue is that of overwhelming supply. In other words, why bother trying to rescue women and children from forced prostitution when they will quickly and simply be replaced by other vulnerable citizens. Such an argument is surprisingly common and is used as a justification for all manner of indifference and inaction. Typically, rather than small-scale interventions that rely on the individual cases of the victims involved, the need for the eradication of global poverty and unilateral debt relief is deemed to be a more crucial first step.

Global poverty and sex trafficking, however, affect one person at a time, and while it is true that two or three girls rescued from a brothel in Southeast Asia can be quickly replaced, for the rescued victims and their families, their lives will be dramatically transformed forever. In addition, every successful intervention costs the criminals involved in trafficking a huge amount of money. Every successful prosecution costs them even more time and valuable resources. Every criminal sentenced to jail changes a community's and a culture's understanding of what is and is not acceptable.

Ultimately, though, I found that the easiest way to silence such pretensions was to ask the advocates of such a position what efforts they would go to should their own wife, sister, daughter, niece or granddaughter be tricked or forced into prostitution. How far would they go and how much money would they spend to invade a brothel where their own flesh and blood was being held captive?

Traveling throughout Southeast Asia, I was routinely told by locals and expats alike that trying to rescue trafficked women and children was a waste of time, and that I should be focusing instead on community development in the villages where the victims were recruited.

There is some truth to this. Where the standard of living is raised and grinding poverty is eliminated, desperation levels are reduced and families are less likely to take the risk of allowing their daughters to seek employment far from home. In the end both community development and prevention efforts at the source, as well as appropriate intervention efforts at the destination, are required to effectively combat sexual slavery.

A further criticism was leveled at one of my employers because of the Christian worldview the organization is based on. There was a general suspicion that we were actively seeking to impose our own morality on other nations and that it was a purely Western or American form of justice we were seeking. Rather than detracting from our work, I maintained that by honestly acknowledging and being open and upfront about what motivated us, our work had credibility and integrity.

When it came to the individual cases of injustice and exploitation, I always explained that we did not rely on any kind of international law or Christian definition of justice, but only the professional application and enforcement of those laws indigenous to the country we were operating in.

Every intervention report completed by the organization contained a section devoted to the local laws and statutes relevant to the criminal offense in question. Before approaching local authorities and asking for their help, we always completed a professional summary of how their own laws applied to those particular criminal actions we had documented.

ENTRAPMENT

As a police officer I was also very aware of the criminal defense of entrapment. As the word suggests, this is what happens when, rather than documenting criminal activity that is already occurring, the investigator instigates or creates the offense and then facilitates the arrest of those responsible. For example, suppose I were to approach someone who was not involved in such exploitation and offer him or her money to procure a child for me and then have the person arrested. This would be deemed unfair by most criminal courts, and the relevant charges would in all likelihood be dismissed.

For this reason I was always careful to ensure that I did not introduce the offense but only documented and recorded crimes already taking place. This was another benefit of having a covert camera record all of my conversations: by the time the matter went before a criminal court, it was clear to all concerned that I had merely participated in what was already an ongoing criminal enterprise.

This did not stop the various defense lawyers and local politicians with vested interests from claiming that we were using our perceived status as wealthy Westerners to secure the arrest of vulnerable and unsuspecting locals within their community.

Another equally common tactic used by defense lawyers during more than one trial was to cross-examine me as to the relevant authority I had exercised in documenting the activities of criminals in a nation that was not my own. If they were able to somehow show that I had no authority to conduct my investigative activities, they could try to persuade the respective court that any evidence I had obtained should therefore be considered inadmissible.

It was in these circumstances that I was especially thankful for three United Nations documents. The first is the United Nations' "Convention on the Rights of the Child," adopted in 1990. Of particular relevance are the following two articles:

Article 34

States Parties undertake to protect the child from all forms of sexual exploitation and sexual abuse. For these purposes, States Parties shall in particular take all appropriate national, bilateral and multilateral measures to prevent:

(a) The inducement or coercion of a child to engage in any unlawful sexual activity;

(b) The exploitative use of children in prostitution or other unlawful sexual practices;

(c) The exploitative use of children in pornographic performances and materials.

Article 35

States Parties shall take all appropriate national, bilateral and multilateral measures to prevent the abduction of, the sale of or traffic in children for any purpose or in any form.

The second document was the 1998 "Declaration on the Right and Responsibility of Individuals, Groups and Organs of Society to Promote and Protect Universally Recognized Human Rights and Fundamental Freedoms." This declaration affirms the rights of individuals and organizations to "know, seek, obtain, receive and hold information about all human rights and fundamental freedoms" and to "make the public more aware of questions relating to all human rights and fundamental freedoms through activities such as education, training and research."

The third was the 2001 "United Nations Convention against Transnational Organized Crime." The convention has, as part of its content, protocols to "Prevent, Suppress and Punish Trafficking in Persons, Especially Women and Children." It states that "effective action to prevent and combat trafficking in persons, especially women and children, requires a comprehensive international approach in the countries of origin, transit and destination that includes measures to prevent such trafficking, to punish the traffickers and to protect the victims of such trafficking."

Organizations and individuals working around the world on the front lines of human rights are often critical of the United Nations for its work (or lack of it) and for the bureaucracy that can sometimes render its good intentions worthless. In my case, I was thankful that every country I worked in was a signatory to one or more of these conventions, declarations and protocols. By pointing the presiding judicial authority to the relevant document that had been endorsed and ratified by their own governments, we were, as an organization, able to further the rights of some of the most vulnerable and exploited people on earth.

I had a growing sense that no matter what I did in pursuit of the goals of the organizations I worked for, there would always be people who were only too willing to criticize our efforts. Ultimately I learned to shut out their vociferous voices and focus on the task at hand. In many respects it was easier for me to do so than some of my administrative colleagues back in America, because I was the one who got to look into the tortured eyes of terrified children and defiled women. And I was so very thankful to have a role to play in bringing them hope.

5

United States

Her Name Is Jeni

In the land of the free and the home of the brave, more than one hundred years after Abraham Lincoln's Emancipation Proclamation, slavery is still alive and well. I found a large brothel that rivals some of the darkest places in the Third World for its corruption, political indifference and overt sexual exploitation. Its name is Las Vegas.

Las Vegas is a city that thrives on the prostitution of children and the trafficking of women. Organized crime, along with an international network of pimps, escort agencies and Internet businesses, fuel the multibillion dollar industry that ensnares thousands of victims every year in its web of lust, greed and deception.

The sex industry in Las Vegas is enormous. Since gambling was first legalized in 1931, sex has been used to promote the city. Indeed it is impossible for any visitor to ignore the intense marketing and the very overt advertising of the sex industry. Huge glossy mobile billboards of half-naked women troll up and down the four-mile strip past the roving eyes of the millions of tourists that flock here each year.

Latino immigrants block the footpaths and sidewalks thrusting colored photographs of scantily clad women into the hands of anyone who will take them. The telephone numbers of very attractive, partially naked women, as well as their going prices, are clearly displayed, and interested clients are assured of discretion and anonymity. And within every home and inside every hotel room are hundreds of yellow pages thick with fronts for prostitution.

SLIDING SCALE

Prostitution at the high end of the scale occurs in all of the major bars and nightclubs in Las Vegas. It is part of a very organized, carefully calculated and meticulously planned criminal enterprise that sends women from one side of the country to the other in pursuit of large entertainment events and conferences. Many high-end prostitutes who want to get access to specific bars or clubs pay hundreds of dollars to the security staff to allow them entry.

One security guard admitted that he typically went home each night with between $2,000 to $4,000 in tips alone, all from prostitutes wanting to get access to the high rollers partying in his club. If the CEO of a big company or a well-known actor or sportsman was visiting his club, the guard would call the girls he knew and alert them. He would then charge the girls $300 to get inside, knowing that if successful, they would each be paid much more by the high rollers. In the city where money reigns, another guard admitted that he regularly let underage girls into his club to sell themselves, because they tipped him well.

Having gained access to a casino or club, the commercial seduction that occurs in Las Vegas is a fine art known as "table surfing." Prostitutes walk from one table to another, carefully looking at what the male patrons are drinking and who they are with. If a man is standing by the bar with one drink he is quickly discounted. However if a male patron is sitting down at a table (tables cost up to $300 or more in some clubs) and has a few bottles of expensive alcohol, then he is considered worthy of attention. The ultimate target is known locally as a "whale," someone who is spending more than a million dollars each night. Hotel staff, casino and bar employees all make money from prostitutes by facilitating their access to such a large catch.

The taxi companies in Las Vegas act as one of the main conduits between the client and the sex industry. Taxi drivers earn many thousands of dollars in additional profit by agreeing to take their lonely male customers to prearranged brothels. By acting as low-level pimps, some cab drivers and limousine services make more than $100,000 a year.

Every weekend thousands of exotic dancers and strippers arrive from out of town to work in the bars, brothels and clubs. Primarily from California, these women make some quick and easy money by staying in a cheap apartment or motel over the weekend and earning up to $3,000 in one night. Sadly also arriving every weekend are girls as young as eleven years old, recruited and forced into prostitution by their pimps.

The high-end prostitutes are at the top of a sliding scale. Further down the Vegas scale of deprivation are the "carpet hos," those women lucky enough to be allowed entry into the casinos, hotels, clubs and bars. They typically work for a pimp or for one of the large escort agencies. Danielle, a stunning black woman with a beautiful smile, was a prime example of this sort of prostitute. Although not the target of my investigation into trafficking, Danielle's story helped me understand a lot of what was happening in Las Vegas.

Danielle was seventeen years old when she first started working as a prostitute. Like a lot of girls from her impoverished neighborhood in Pittsburgh, Danielle began turning tricks just to make the money she needed to get clothes or to get her hair done. She said it was very common for young black girls to sell themselves to pay their bills. She was an A student in high school and then went on to college for two years. She sold her body when she needed quick and easy money.

Danielle said it was peer pressure and the desire for more money that led her to Las Vegas at the age of twenty. Sadly, one of her first experiences was being kidnapped, raped and imprisoned in a hotel room with her client for three days. She eventually managed to escape, and the offender was later arrested and charged by the police. Since then she had been quick to learn the rules of the game, such as always using protection, making the client pay first and never going with more than one man at a time.

Speaking to her after four years in Vegas, she said she found the work sickening and was tired of doing tricks. She had no sex drive, did not get excited by any man, and her body had stopped responding to any kind of stimulation. Indeed she described finding it disgusting to be with a client, saying that it made her feel sick talking about the many things they wanted to do with her. Whether the man was very handsome or had a great body made absolutely no difference. All she wanted was the money and to get out of there as quickly as she could.

As I delved a little deeper, Danielle admitted that she was in fact repulsed by and detested her clients. With tears in her eyes, she expressed her anger toward those who so casually used her. Sometimes while performing oral sex on a client, Danielle found herself wondering whether she should bite it off or not. "Ask any hooker in Las Vegas," she said. "If they are honest, they will tell you that if someone is giving them money just to screw them, then at the first opportunity they are going to screw them back." Danielle said a lot of her clients had wives staying with them in Vegas, and they liked the idea of having sex with her while their wives were staying in another room.

Danielle said that everything about Las Vegas was a lie, including the prostitution. However, despite the hatred she expressed toward her clients, she admitted that she found it difficult to leave because the money was addictive. On a good night she could make more than $2,000.

At the other end of the Vegas scale are the women and children who line the back streets of the city, away from the bright lights and security cameras. These women and children typically come from abusive and impoverished backgrounds from all over the country. Some are runaways, and many have been forced into prostitution in their early teens. I paid for the time of one such street worker and found that she was no exception. Jane was white, attractive, twenty-four years old and had been working the streets of Las Vegas for two years.

Originally from Kansas, Jane's mother was a prostitute and drug addict. Jane and her younger sister lived with her mother and her pimp, named Jeremy. When she was six years old, Jeremy began molesting Jane and her sister. Her mother knew about the abuse but was so addicted she did not have the ability or the conscience to do anything about it. Jeremy first raped Jane when she was seven, and he began pimping her on the streets when she was thirteen.

Jane described the huge demand for her sexual services at the age of thirteen. She had a couple of regular customers who paid her $600-$700 for sex because she was so young. She used the money to pay the rent and to care for her younger sister. Making money for Jeremy was the only way he would feed and clothe the family.

When her younger sister was eight, Jane's mother sold her to another pimp to get money for drugs. Jane then ran away from home. At the age of fourteen she ended up in Phoenix, where she began working as a stripper. She then fell pregnant to the man who was pimping her at the time and subsequently gave birth to a daughter. She continued to work on the street during her entire pregnancy and came to Las Vegas so she could support her child.

Like Danielle, Jane's circumstances did not fall within the strict definition of human trafficking, and so I did not pursue her any further. However both women were typical of those I met during the course of my investigation. They walked the streets of Las Vegas simply because, at some point in their lives, they had been enslaved and ensnared by others who had used them for their own predatory gain.

ILLEGAL BROTHELS

In the suburbs of Las Vegas I found a large number of brothels that cater solely to Latino immigrants. They are very difficult to penetrate by the law enforcement community because they only allow Latino men to enter and the girls sold there are moved regularly from one place to another. Operated by Latino gangs, these brothels are very discreet and well-organized. Along with other criminal entrepreneurs, the gangs had discovered just how lucrative it could be to sell their "products" over and over again. Their businesses involved much less risk than drug dealing, and it was common knowledge that even if prosecuted, the average prison time for selling women was far less than for other crimes.

The first opportunity I had to infiltrate such criminal activity came at the hands of a greedy taxi driver. A local television documentary crew had only recently exposed the pimping activities of many of the main taxi companies, so the drivers were particularly cautious. However my Kiwi accent convinced one particular driver that I could not possibly be part of the law enforcement community. When I made it clear that I was feeling especially eager for sex, he pulled over to the side of the road and began making some telephone calls on my behalf. A few moments later, we were heading across town to a very nondescript apartment complex in the suburbs.

After parking some distance away from the destination, my driver walked with me to the front door. He was eager to get his cut of the $350 I had been told my encounter would cost. As the door opened I stepped into the very familiar environment of a brothel, its seemingly timeless ritual reenacted all over the world. As the Asian female manager ushered me into the living room, I could have been anywhere in the world. In a manner befitting the universal tale of male domination, five women, all in their early twenties, lined up in front of me wearing only their underwear and smiling warmly. The manager explained that I could have my choice of Japanese, Thai, Korean, Chinese or Latino.

Doing what, by now, had almost become second nature to me, I quickly scanned the women before me, searching their eyes and their body language for any telltale sign that would help me correctly identify the slaves among them. As I returned their smiles I searched for the nervous glance toward the manager, a less than authentic smile, deference to the other girls or fear in their eyes. When I chose the girl from Korea, the others quietly disappeared from the room as I paid my driver. Giving me his business card he offered to return and pick me up for the return ride to my hotel.

JENI'S STORY

Taking me by the hand my Korean liaison led me to a bedroom in the house and shut the door behind her. She explained that I had to first pay her $300, which would go to the "house," and that anything I paid on top of that was a tip she was entitled to keep. I quickly built a rapport with the girl, who said her working name was Jeni. She explained that she had traveled to the United States from Seoul four years earlier after a girlfriend contacted her and offered her a well-paying sales job. She arrived only to find out that the sale was of her own body and that her prospective employers were very sophisticated criminals. Jeni was told that she had to work for one year in the industry before she could begin making her own money and get a Western boyfriend.

Jeni said she lived in Los Angeles but was shuttled back and forth between her home and Las Vegas. She was not allowed to leave the house, commenced work at 10 a.m. each day and continued to work through the night as long as there were willing customers. When asked if I could meet her for lunch at a later date,

Jeni said she might be allowed to do so, but only after getting permission from her manager and then only for one hour. The tight controls surrounding her every move, the restrictions placed on her freedom, the financial debt imposed on her along with the deception used to bring her to the United States all pointed to human trafficking.

When Jeni removed her clothing and indicated that she was ready, I carefully explained that in my own culture it was customary to get to know a woman before having sex with her. I asked her for a massage instead, and used this as an opportunity to get additional information while setting up an excuse to meet her again in the future. Accepting my request, Jeni continued to quietly whisper her regrets and share her feelings with me as she massaged my back as best she could with her untrained hands. By the time my hour was up, I had a more complete picture of how the brothel operated and who was in charge.

Returning to the living room, I spoke again with the manager and asked if I could return at a later date. Having established myself as a legitimate customer in her mind, she quickly agreed and wrote down a telephone number I could call in the future. Handing me her card, she said her name was Kate. Kate further agreed to consider my request to meet Jeni for lunch and invited me to call the following day.

While she telephoned my taxi driver, I noted six or seven cell phones spread out on the dining room table. Each phone represented a different advertisement, possibly even a different company name, listed in one of the many places where potential clients would look. A black man in his thirties was quietly working away on a computer in a corner of the room. As he did so, I saw that he was also monitoring a large television screen, which showed the exterior of the building from several different angles provided by security cameras discreetly positioned outside.

PAK'S STORY

Having said my farewells I was quick to invent and communicate a story of sexual conquest to my faithful but greedy driver as we drove back toward the Vegas strip. Seizing the opportunity to utilize the services and knowledge of my new friend, I asked if he knew of any other places where I could continue to live out my fantasies for the evening. After a few further telephone calls, we were heading toward a new destination.

Pulling into a 7-Eleven parking lot, my driver explained that he had to park away from the next address as a precaution. A few moments later a late-model Lexus SUV pulled alongside us and a smartly dressed Asian woman invited me to get into her vehicle. I arranged to meet my driver back at the 7-Eleven when I was finished. The woman indicated that her English was not very good. She then drove me to a modern single-story home only a few blocks away.

After we pulled into the driveway, an iron gate swung shut behind us. After asking me to follow her, she escorted me to the front door where an Asian man in his late twenties was waiting. He led me past the main living room where I saw another Asian man was seated. After walking down a short hallway he opened the door to a small bedroom. I walked inside and was greeted by a shy Asian girl in her late teens wearing only a bikini.

As the door closed behind us, the girl introduced herself as Pak. She could not speak much English and it quickly became apparent that communication was going to be a challenge. She said she was from Korea and that there were girls from both Korea and China available if I wanted.

Pak was clearly more nervous than Jeni had been, and she was eager to initiate sexual contact with me. When I tried to slow her down and continued to ask her questions, she became perplexed and then asked suspiciously if I was a policeman. Laughing this off, I accepted her back massage, which seemed to put her at ease.

I then declined anything further on the basis that I was not feeling well and paid her for her time.

As I walked back into the living room, I saw two other young Asian women wearing bikinis leave their room with an Asian man aged in his fifties. After thanking Pak, I walked back outside to where the shining Lexus and my escort was waiting. Without saying a word the woman returned me to the parking lot of the 7-Eleven. As I arrived, a black chauffeur-driven limousine pulled in beside us. I watched as discreetly as possible as the Asian woman approached the vehicle and spoke to the occupant. The dark-tinted windows hid the identity of the wealthy man seated in the rear of the car, but his presence indicated his intentions.

The arrival of my taxi prevented me from observing anything further, and I duly headed back to one of the hotels on the strip, where I had said I was staying. I was pleased with what I had discovered and with the intelligence I had gathered during the course of the night. I was also incredibly sad. Having spent more than six years living in the United States I considered it my second home. Many of its citizens were among my closest family and friends. I knew no country was immune from human trafficking, but finding it so blatantly displayed on my own back door were two very different things.

FBI RAID

The following day I met with a special agent from the FBI Organized Crime Division and a detective from the criminal intelligence section of the Las Vegas Metropolitan Police Department. Both men worked closely on Asian organized crime in Las Vegas and were part of a joint task force. They were very receptive and grateful for the information I was able to provide them. They confirmed that the first address I had visited was one of several addresses they were targeting as part of a much larger operation. I learned that the Chinese Madame had a gambling addiction and that her husband was connected to a gang making child pornography.

They were, however, unaware of the prostitution occurring at the second address. Officers from their task force had put surveillance on the house about one month previously due to a major illegal narcotics operation being run through the address by Chinese organized crime. They were not aware that they were now also clearly involved in human trafficking and prostitution. As we talked openly about what I had so relatively easily discovered, I learned that there were more than ten such illegal brothels selling Asian women, all operating less than one mile from the bright lights of the Las Vegas strip.

While the information I provided was useful, it clearly formed only a very small part of a much larger targeted and intelligence-driven operation being patiently and professionally pieced together by local law enforcement. Rather than risk jeopardizing these efforts, I indicated that I would not conduct any further investigations and opted to leave the preparation and planning of any future intervention in their hands.

I later learned that the Las Vegas FBI eventually raided the two locations along with seven others. Eight people were arrested as the culmination of a two-year operation code-named "Doll House." Twenty-four women from Asia, South America and Eastern Europe were also found at the addresses. The principal offenders were charged with living off the earnings of prostitution and drug trafficking.

Unfortunately, none of the prostitutes were willing to indicate that there was any kind of coercion or deception involved, so trafficking charges were not laid. However, many of the women could not speak English and were later deported for being in the United States illegally.

"What happens in Vegas stays in Vegas." Downtown Las Vegas, unlike many other brothels around the world, has its share of bright lights, amazing architecture and exceptional entertainment. But at the end of the day it is just another brothel.

FACTS: *Internet*

- The exponential growth of the sex-trafficking industry can partly be attributed to the ease with which people from anywhere can meet and exchange information. The Internet is the fastest growing communication network in the world. Because Internet communication is unregulated, it has led to an escalation of the global sex trade and the commercial sexual exploitation of women and children.

- Professor Donna Hughes at the University of Rhode Island researches trafficking and sexual exploitation, and states:

  > The Internet has facilitated the creation of online communities that are virtually free from outside interference or laws. With little fear of detection, apprehension or punishment, men can now buy, sell, auction, degrade, humiliate, torture, stalk, view, consume, and dispose of women at their leisure.
  >
  > The pimps and buyers on the Internet are funding the development and expansion of the commercial Internet. . . . The [IT] industry publicly avoids acknowledging or denies the influence of the pornographers and pimps on the Internet industry because the two have become dependent on one another and are now collaborators. All the large Internet service providers are dependent on the sex industry for their profits.

- The Internet is the preferred marketing location for mail-order brides, live strip shows and overseas sex tours. The profits are astronomical, and few effective barriers exist. With little regulation the traffickers and promoters of sexual exploitation can utilize the Internet for their own criminal purposes.

- The Internet has rendered national borders meaningless. Lawmakers and law enforcers worldwide have been left scrambling while organized criminal syndicates have used the Internet to their advantage, displaying all forms of sexual exploitation and recruiting unsuspecting women.

6

Dangerous

To live is to risk dying. To hope is to risk despair.
To try is to risk failure. But risks must be taken because the greatest hazard in
life is to risk nothing. The person who risks nothing,
does nothing, has nothing and is nothing. They may avoid suffering and
sorrow, but they cannot learn, feel, change, grow, love, live.
Chained by their certitudes, they are as a slave, they have forfeited their
freedom. Only a person who risks is free.

Anonymous

Not far from my home in New Zealand is a beautiful winding river that was made famous through the filming of Peter Jackson's movie trilogy *The Lord of the Rings*. The Ford of Rivendell was the place where the dark riders, called the Nazgûl, charged the heroine Arwen as she ferried the wounded Frodo across to safety on her horse. Those familiar with *The Fellowship of the Ring* will recall that it was here that Arwen turned to face the evil horsemen before she called on the magical powers of the area to raise the river and wash the Nazgûl away.

As a young boy I spent many hours during the summer holidays exploring the same rivers, valleys, lakes and mountains that were to later become the majestic backdrops to the perilous escapes, violent battles and breathtaking adventure in *The Lord of the Rings*. Lost in my own imagination I would often be found brandishing a rifle and charging some enemy outpost hidden high among the rocks and the tussock grass. The rabbits and hares I found there would beat a hasty retreat into the distance before turning to watch me with bemusement as I raised my weapon above my head and yelled in victory.

In his bestselling book *Wild at Heart*, author John Eldredge wrote:

> Life is not a problem to be solved; it is an adventure to be lived. That's the nature of it and has been since the beginning when God set the dangerous stage for this high stakes drama and called the whole wild enterprise good. He rigged the world in such a way that it only works when we embrace risk as the theme of our lives, which is to say, only when we live by faith. A man won't be happy until he's got adventure in his work, in his love and in his spiritual life.

It was in pursuit of just such an adventure that, like Frodo, I later set out from Middle-earth to travel into the dark lands of Mordor and to destroy the power of evil that was seeking to enslave and bind so many. I knew it would involve risk. I knew it would involve danger. But I was adamant that the greater danger lay in *not* doing that which made me come alive. I was more afraid of living behind the bars of a cage made of safety and control, and to discover only too late that the opportunity to do great deeds with courage and passion had passed me by.

ESCAPING SAFETY

During my time in Southeast Asia I had the opportunity to work alongside several members of the special forces (SF) community. These are highly trained, elite members of various branches of the military. They are men who carry themselves with the strength and confidence that only comes from having conquered their fears and their enemies. They live on the extreme edge. I was always thankful for their assistance and felt much safer with them around. I knew better than to try to be anything other than authentic with these soldiers, and I instinctively respected them for their courage, their endurance and their skill.

I was pleasantly surprised by the respect and affection they communicated to me, and I endeavored to live up to their expectations of me as a consummate professional. However, sometimes the differences in our training and life experiences became glaringly obvious.

On one such occasion I was in the company of two such men who, as a courtesy, had offered to assist me in infiltrating a very dangerous group of organized criminals in Southeast Asia. When I explained that the only defensive weapon I would be carrying was a small collapsible baton, one of the men showed me a small black-handled knife with a curved steel blade and a finger hole in the handle. The "bear claw," he explained, was lightweight, razor sharp and perfect for self-defense. He showed me how to hold the knife while slicing the blade across the unprotected throat of an assailant.

When I expressed some discomfort at the thought of having to rip someone's throat open, the steely-eyed veteran of combat paused before looking me in the eye and said, "If it is you or them, never, never hesitate."

I explained that police officers in New Zealand are unarmed and that all of the training I had received to date was focused on how to use the least possible force to defend myself. One of the men quoted the motto of his particular branch of the special forces, saying there are only "the quick and the dead." The second man cited his motto, "strength and honor." The immense gulf between us became apparent when, in response, I quoted the motto of the New Zealand Police: "safer communities together." The silence that followed said it all.

THE UNTHINKABLE BUSINESS OFFER

The first time I was very thankful to be carrying a collapsible baton was during my initial deployment to a country in Southeast Asia. Inside the dark interior of one of the many brothels, I had asked to see what girls the manager had available. In his late thirties, the man arrogantly ignored Yem, my translator, when he attempted to interpret for me. In broken English the brothel owner proudly communicated that he had learned to speak English while studying to be a missionary at a Bible college in the United States. He said his name was Rangsey, and he invited us to follow him to a room at the rear of the building.

Due to their illegal trade in humans, some of the brothel managers were in the habit of padlocking the sliding steel doors of their brothels once the customer had entered. This was to prevent any outside intervention from interrupting the illegal activity and abuse occurring inside. It was a particularly unnerving practice for me, given that at any time my true identity could be discovered. Locking the doors meant that I had no escape route. It also meant that no one could assist me as, most of the time, no one even knew where I was. I was thankful that Rangsey did not adopt this policy, and I made a mental note of how to return to the front door and exit the building if necessary.

We knew from the intelligence we had received from our special-forces associates that there were firearms in the village. As a result of civil war during the 1970s, a large amount of weapons and military ordinance remained in the hands of the people. To this day, one of the most popular tourist activities in the area is to throw a hand grenade, fire a machine gun or shoot a rocket launcher. The local criminals involved in human trafficking were known to have access to many of these weapons. I therefore had to assume that Rangsey and the other criminals operating their very profitable businesses inside the village also had access.

Rangsey disappeared briefly; when he returned, he had a small

Vietnamese girl with him. Only five or six years old, the girl was wearing a bright, pretty dress and her black hair was neatly tied up into two small pigtails. Looking up at me with her large dark eyes, she seemed accustomed to being summoned to the room to fulfill the dark fantasies of foreign men. Rangsey explained that it would cost $30 to have the girl perform oral sex on me. The covert camera I was wearing silently recorded all that was being said, and I knew that Rangsey had just committed a crime for which he could go to jail for a very long time.

In keeping with my cover I offered to pay Rangsey a deposit for the sexual services of the little girl, and I also inquired about the possibility of using his premises for the proposed rendezvous. "Why not?" he replied. The former apprentice missionary seemed quite excited by the prospect and, again, rather arrogantly indicated that he could handle any request.

Rangsey then looked me in the eye and said that, in order to complete our business agreement, I must first have sex with the little girl standing before me. Once that was done, he said, anything was possible.

I quickly assessed my options. I considered taking the child into one of the bedrooms as I had done in some of the other brothels and pass the time by finding out as much as I could about her background and true identity. However I sensed in Rangsey a ruthlessness and a level of suspicion I had not previously encountered inside the village. I suspected that my encounter with the girl would be carefully monitored in some way, or at the very least that the child would be interrogated afterward as to what actually took place between us.

I chose instead to maintain that I was simply the tour manager and that I had no sexual interest myself in small children. Rangsey visibly changed at this point, and his careful gaze swept over my entire body. He repeated his demand that I must have sex with the girl before he would trust me and engage in any ongoing business relationship with me. I called his bluff by asking for an older girl, hoping that this request would satisfy his growing concern about my stated intention for being in the village.

Instead, Rangsey quickly dismissed the small girl and, after carefully looking at me once again, he very calmly said he suspected I was working for a human rights organization. He demanded to see some form of identification and insisted that he search me. He pointed at me and demanded to see what I was carrying in my pockets. I behaved as if I was upset that he should question my integrity, and I asked my translator to explain my business to him.

Yem spoke rapidly to Rangsey in his own language, and although I don't know what was said, I do know he was very convincing. This was because, at that stage, Yem still believed that I was in fact a sex tourist, and he had already seen me conduct numerous other transactions of a similar nature.

Whatever Yem said was enough to give Rangsey pause and to question whether, in fact, he might be missing out on a potentially lucrative business opportunity. However, he repeated his demand that I have sex with a child before we could proceed. I refused, and looking at Yem, I said that we would take our business elsewhere. As I stepped forward to leave, Rangsey moved forward to block my path. Looking me in the eye, he carefully scrutinized me once more, searching for whatever telltale signs might confirm his suspicions. In a calm but clear voice, he then said very matter-of-factly, "You come back here, I kill you."

With resignation on my face and with every ounce of self-control I could muster, I slowly made my way back to the front of the brothel, pausing to say hello to some of the older prostitutes as I did so. If I did or said anything that confirmed Rangsey's suspicions in any way, I knew it was unlikely that I would reach the front door alive. Yem and I were just about to step from the dark interior into the bright sunlight outside when I heard Rangsey's voice immediately behind me quietly repeat, "You come back here, I kill you."

Yem had become my right-hand man and was now intricately involved in all of the business transactions I had made to date with the various criminals inside the village. If we were going to rescue any of the victims and apprehend any of the perpetrators, it was imperative that Yem remained convinced of my authenticity. With this in mind, I suggested we go and see one of the other pimps in the village. This other pimp carried himself with authority and many of the other younger pimps seemed to look up to him. His name was Kosal.

When I conveyed through Yem what had happened with Rangsey, Kosal became very upset and began talking about retribution. He suggested that he send his boys over to burn Rangsey's house down. I thanked Kosal for his support and played the role of nursing my damaged pride. However, I asked him not to do anything to Rangsey and simply said it would ultimately mean more business for Kosal and the others. I left the village disappointed that my cover had so nearly been blown. However I was confident that by speaking to Kosal first, I had thwarted any attempts Rangsey might make to persuade others in the village not to deal with me.

When I returned to the village a few days later, I entered with some trepidation, not knowing whether the words of Rangsey or Kosal carried more weight among the criminal fraternity. Even seeing Kosal walking toward me with a big smile did not put me completely at ease, as I imagined this man could smile just as widely while slitting my throat. However Kosal was eager to inform me that some of his "boys" had given Rangsey a beating. Kosal said Rangsey would learn from the black eyes and broken nose he had received that he should not try to smear my good reputation again. Kosal further confirmed that everyone else in the village was still more than willing to do business with me.

Kosal was subsequently arrested during a police raid and was later sentenced to more than ten years imprisonment. Rangsey fled the village and was not seen again. Neither was the small girl with pigtails.

A FINGERNAIL AWAY FROM DEATH

Ultimately it was in a country in southernmost Asia where I came closest to being discovered and eliminated. I was preparing to leave the largest of several brothels, each one operated and tightly controlled by a ruthless group of organized criminals. I had successfully captured sufficient evidence on my covert camera to prosecute many of those present, and I was eager to escape with the evidence, as well as my life, intact. The camera I wore was an older model that was eventually discontinued by its manufacturer. This was because, after operating the camera for long periods, the lens became extremely hot. This was obviously very undesirable for anyone working undercover.

Given my job description it was sometimes extremely challenging to communicate in an open and uninhibited manner with those women trying to touch and otherwise seduce me while, at the same time, ensuring that none of them touched that particular part of my body where the camera lens was located. Anyone touching it would immediately become curious as to what was creating so much heat on my body. I had little in the way of an answer to satisfy any such questions.

On this particular occasion it had been necessary to let the camera run for some time to record the most compelling evidence. Having said my goodbyes to the girls and the principal trafficker inside the brothel, the manager led me to the rear of the building where several guards were stationed on the inside and outside of a large steel door. While he was saying something to his security guards, the manager quickly looked outside to make sure the way was clear for me to leave. I moved forward to walk past him but as I did so, unaware that I had begun to move forward, the manager raised his arm and brought it back toward me in an apparent attempt to wave me on. The back of his hand came to rest on my shirt directly on top of the hot lens.

Time stood still and my heart missed a beat. A thousand thoughts flooded my mind, as I stood frozen in my step. As the manager turned slowly to face me, I wondered whether this was one of those times I should "not hesitate," and I mentally prepared to fight my way out.

I anticipated the ugly scowl of a man who had suddenly identified his enemy. What I saw instead was the friendly face of someone still blissfully unconcerned. As he put out his arm to shake my hand it took every ounce of self-control to walk on past him in an unhurried manner, through the doorway and away from the brothel. As I walked away from the building, it took some time for my heart rate to return to normal. To this day I can only surmise that the top of his fingernail rested on the hot camera lens, thereby preventing him from sensing its telltale heat. Or perhaps I was experiencing protection from the Rescuer.

HOT SEAT

Thankfully not all of the danger I faced was as life-threatening. During my second deployment to Southeast Asia, I was asked to test one of the early covert camera systems. We used a variety of suppliers and covert recording devices, and each time an improvement was made, we had to test the equipment to determine its suitability and reliability. On this occasion an extra battery pack had been added to the camera system in an effort to extend the recording-time capability.

The targets I had been given were brothels selling underage women and children. Because of this, they were extremely paranoid about people bringing any kind of camera or cell phone into their premises. In addition there was a concern that some patrons might bring weapons into the building. For these reasons, the brothel management took the unusual step of having security guards physically search each of the potential customers as they lined up at the doorway. I was not worried about the camera lens being detected, as it was very small and well concealed. But I did not want to get caught trying to enter the facility with the recording device itself, because, in addition to being dangerous, such a discovery could potentially thwart any future operation.

I made an additional effort in concealing the extra battery pack and recorder so it was flush with my skin and buried under my clothing. I was confident that I would be able to smuggle the camera system inside the target building and capture the necessary video evidence.

It was well after dark on the night of the operation when I approached the several guards standing outside the brothel. I engaged in casual conversation and tried to appear calm as the gorilla of a man guarding the door carefully patted me down. Thankfully he did not find the camera, and it was with a degree of satisfaction and smugness that I sauntered into the brothel and sat at the bar.

I quickly identified some potential victims and I used a wireless remote in my pocket to activate the covert camera. I then began recording a conversation with one of the owners. It was during this time that things began to get interesting.

As noted earlier, the one drawback associated with our early-model cameras was their propensity to get extremely hot within a very short space of time. I began to realize this slight oversight on my part when the recorder and battery pack, along with the wires connecting the system, all began to overheat. In an effort to bring the transaction to a hasty end, I began to talk faster and faster and tried as unobtrusively as possible to maneuver the electronic baggage away from my skin, which by this stage was starting to burn.

I hoped and prayed that the criminals I was speaking to only suspected I was suffering from some kind of illness as I began to perspire rapidly and look increasingly uncomfortable. It was with considerable self-control that I restrained myself from ripping my clothes off. I eventually extricated myself from the negotiations and walked outside and toward my parked vehicle. Once inside my car and under the cover of darkness, I tore at my clothes and removed the offending electronics.

My final evaluation report strongly rejected the latest series of camera modifications.

7

Southeast Asia

Her Name Is Mahal

"She's eighteen, right?!"

The sharp nasal accent of the tall Australian cut through the incessant beat and neon lights of the go-go bar. Placing his finger across his lips to indicate that her real age should remain a secret, he winked and returned to his office at the rear of the club. His club. But she was not eighteen. She was probably only twelve years old. She sat beside me wearing only a fluorescent bikini, her undeveloped breasts barely filling the small bra cups.

Mahal had been at the bar for only two weeks. Her mother was a local widow who suffered from chronic health problems. With no means of support, Mahal and her three other siblings were all desperate to try to earn enough money to support their struggling family. The southern city of Luton thrives on the desperation of vulnerable girls, and Matthew Thompson, the Australian bar owner, was just one of many who was only too willing to turn Mahal's desperation into his profit.

Together with his wife, Thompson owned a go-go bar called Flamingo. The club was one of more than a hundred similar establishments that lined both sides of the main street. Originally established to service the demand created by the many American servicemen based at the nearby naval base, the district had become known internationally as a place where the girls were "willing, cheap and young."

Along with an American colleague, I had spent a week bar hopping, documenting those bars that were selling underage girls. While each had a different name (School House, Paradise, Mermaids), they were all essentially the same. Each bar was shrouded in varying degrees of darkness, with thumping music and strobe lights providing sufficient illumination to see the products available for purchase. Those products were Filipino women and children, all dressed in bikinis, many topless and most wearing a card with a number on it to make it easier for the clients to choose.

Inside each bar, around the outside of a raised stage where the girls strutted in high-heeled shoes and wrapped themselves around poles, male tourists primarily from the West watched and salivated. Some fit the image of the stereotypical sex tourist: overweight, unattractive and with few social skills. Others looked like men who could easily have been my mechanic, my bank manager, my barber or my neighbor. From their dimly lit tables, they ordered beers to consume and every so often a girl to flirt with. After indicating which number they wanted, the mamasan or female manager sent the chosen girl over to the male client to encourage him to drink more alcohol and then seduce him.

Once the client had inspected the goods and was happy with his choice, he was then required to pay a "bar fine," which would allow him to take the girl back to his hotel. This was usually about $25. A small percentage of this was later paid to the girls themselves, along with any tips given to them by the client.

TRUSTWORTHY POLICE

Having limited the scope of our investigation to four bars selling underage girls, the next challenge was to find authorities we could

trust to do something about it. This was the first time we had conducted an operation in this part of the country, and we did not
have any existing relationships with local law enforcement. Having been told that corruption was endemic in the area, we knew
we would have to proceed carefully.

I had covertly recorded all of my interactions with the perpetrators selling the children, including the cash deposits used to
secure their services. Having gathered the necessary evidence,
the next challenge lay in finding some trustworthy authorities
who would be prepared to act on our information. We made our
initial approach to the federal authorities because, like their
American counterparts, the federal officers had jurisdiction
throughout the country.

The federal investigators were understood to be more trustworthy than the national police in the area. While they welcomed our
information and the additional intelligence it provided them, they
were initially unwilling to act with any urgency. We therefore
played a delicate game of diplomacy by taking the same information to the local police commander responsible for the exploitation of women and children.

While we waited to see which law enforcement agency was
going to agree to work with us, my American colleague and I decided to stay away from the bars. We had become fairly well-
known by some of the owners and managers during our time in
Luton City, and we thought it would be good to keep a low profile
prior to any potential intervention by the authorities.

While staying at a nice hotel in the city, I unwittingly drew unnecessary attention to myself. I had not yet fully grasped the difference between electricity voltage converters and outlet adapter
plugs. These were needed for the myriad of electronic equipment
items we traveled with and used around the world. While trying
to recharge my camera, I plugged an American 110-volt power
strip directly into the wall. Instantly, 220 volts surged through it

with a deafening bang, blowing it apart and sending smoke and wiring across my room.

My colleague in the adjacent hotel room heard the noise, as did most of the hotel. Convinced it was a gunshot he dashed into my room, only to find me with a confused and dazed expression on my face, holding the remains of a smoking power strip. I failed to see the funny side when he collapsed with laughter onto the floor. I duly counted all of my fingers to make sure they were all still attached. The hotel's staff was relieved that nothing sinister had occurred, and aside from my ego, the only permanent damage was a slight charring of the wall outlet.

In the days that followed, while we waited for a response, my colleague had to return to the United States while I remained in the field. When it did not look like any law enforcement action was imminent, my supervisor contacted me from the United States and asked me to try one last time. I returned to speak with the police commander, who gave a favorable response. I then went to see the federal law enforcement director, and when he learned that the police were willing to assist us, he agreed to act on the information straight away and asked me to provide a briefing for his staff later that evening.

BRIEFING

While the number of federal agents in the area was relatively small, each agent had a number of civilian operatives and informants who worked for him. I therefore watched with amazement as about sixty men materialized throughout the evening. I had no idea where they came from or how they had been contacted. Most were dressed in army fatigues and carried an automatic weapon of some kind or a pump-action shotgun. Some of the men seemed a little suspicious of the white foreigner who was responsible for disrupting their evening.

Having been assured that all of the men could understand English, the director invited me to speak to the small army that had formed at the station. I relied on the New Zealand Police briefing model and outlined the situation in Luton City. In order to get the men on my side, I was careful to express my own frustration and anger at seeing adult men from the West walking hand in hand back to their hotels with small local girls. I thought I could see a change in the expressions and the look in the eyes of some of the men gathered. I hoped that they too were angry at the casual exploitation of their own impoverished women and children.

I outlined the mission for the evening, being the rescue of those underage girls being sold for sex and the arrest of the bar owners responsible for their sale. We agreed that I would return to the four targeted bars that evening to purchase the underage girls I had previously documented. These transactions would be witnessed by some of the federal agents who would covertly infiltrate the bars beforehand. I gave cash to some of the agents to spend in the bars to ensure that their cover was authentic. Once each of the girls had been transported back to my hotel and placed in the care of social workers and agents, the remaining staff would then raid each of the four bars simultaneously and apprehend the owners and managers present.

I concluded the briefing by thanking everyone for their willingness to assist and for their cooperation, then handed the meeting over to the director to say a few words. I was pleased with what I had said and thought I had done a good job of briefing those present. I was quietly hopeful that the operation would run smoothly and successfully. I sensed a growing excitement within the group of men gathered, which I mistook to be a desire to see some well-overdue justice done.

However, my perception was shattered a few moments later when the director thought it necessary to explain to his men that they were not to have sex with any of the girls before, during or after the operation. It seemed that at least some of the civilian reinforcements had come with the expectation that infiltrating the go-go bars might involve sex of some kind. As the agents and operatives then began loading their weapons, I recognized a look of disappointment in the eyes of some of those gathered. It was then that I realized that it was going to be a long night and that the rescue of Mahal and the others looked far from certain.

CLUB FLAMINGO

When I entered Club Flamingo, I was relieved to see that Mahal was present. After requesting her services for the evening, I paid the bar fine to the duty manager. Sitting at the bar drinking beer and casually watching the purchase were two undercover agents.

I transported Mahal back to my hotel and then returned to the other four bars and repeated the process. The operation proceeded as planned with the exception that, in two of the four bars, I did not locate some of the children because they had already been purchased for the evening. When all of the girls were secured in my hotel room, the signal was given and the agents raided all of the targeted bars.

Their actions provoked outrage from many of the bar owners, most of whom routinely enjoyed operating without any outside interference from local law enforcement. Nevertheless the agents arrested a number of owners and managers, and removed a number of other girls who appeared to be teenagers and whose age would later have to be verified.

I stayed at the hotel and assisted with the transportation of Mahal and the other girls to the police station. What followed was an eye-opening and extremely frustrating evening for me as to the myriad ways in which an operation and prosecution of this nature can typically falter.

Upon our arrival, several bar owners and managers were already being processed and charged. They included the Australian I had met earlier, Matthew Thompson. The girls who had been

removed from the bars were also present. My first concern was
that the agents were allowing the alleged perpetrators to mingle
and interact freely with the underage victims. I asked that the girls
be placed in a separate room while the suspects were processed.
My concern was that the suspects would threaten or otherwise
direct the girls as to what they should say.

I subsequently found one of the operatives propositioning one
of the thirteen-year-old girls inside one of the interview rooms. He
was clearly intoxicated. With delicate diplomacy I used his own
reputation as a means of rescuing the girl by reminding him that
he should not be alone with her in case she later made up some
kind of false allegation against him. I guided her back to the main
waiting room where she joined the others.

Shortly after, the same operative then approached me and explained that he had purchased a lot more alcohol than I had given
him money for, and he asked for more money to cover his expenses. While trying to control the growing anger inside my stom-
ach, I calmly reassured him that I would cover his expenses later.

With any intervention of this kind, I knew it was imperative to
get the victims cooperation as soon as possible by reassuring them
that they are not the ones being prosecuted. However, some of the
other agents clearly had limited training in this area and little in-
terviewing experience. They proceeded to process the girls as if
they were perpetrators by taking their photographs and finger-
prints. Some agents even began yelling at the girls when they believed they were lying. All this did was ostracize the girls further
and make them more uncooperative.

At the same time, I was alerted by one of the social workers to
the fact that one of the main doors had been left open and that
some of the perpetrators had casually walked outside. We quickly
informed the agents who rushed outside and grabbed the suspects,
who were by this stage casually walking off.

The agents proceeded to take statements from each of the girls.

During this time I went with one of the social workers to a local fast food restaurant and purchased some food for the agents and the girls. The operatives began to drift away into the night. Finally in the early hours of the morning, the statements were completed. The girls began to fall asleep on the chairs and benches scattered around the holding room. A few agents stayed in the station overnight and slept in their offices. The two social workers and I took turns staying awake to monitor the girls.

TEARS

It was during the early hours of the morning that I had the most difficult experience of the entire deployment. Some of the older-looking girls, who had clearly worked in the go-go bars for some time, began mocking and taunting me. They believed that my actions had led to their removal from the bars as well as the associated loss of income. The younger ones picked up this attitude and eventually all of the girls began expressing their frustration and anger by verbally abusing me. "You lied to us," they said. While I maintained an outward veneer of professional calm, inside I began to question all I had believed about this work of rescue.

The emotional turmoil and adrenaline-fueled excitement I had experienced during the last twenty-four hours left me feeling completely exhausted. With the verbal abuse continuing, one of the social workers suggested I take a break. Confused and disheartened I walked outside into the morning heat and found a small tree standing beside the dusty road that led into the station compound. I sat down under the tree and amid thoughts of my wife thousands of miles away, I quietly prayed and cried.

While I did not understand it at the time, what was happening was to become a fairly common occurrence during my work over the next four years. For a variety of reasons, when an intervention is conducted that results in the rescue of a woman or child from sexual slavery, there are often conflicting feelings of loss, shame, isolation or misplaced loyalty to their oppressors, which leave them feeling angry and full of grief.

For others who have worked in the industry for some time, their identities have sometimes become so intertwined with their brothel community and the sex work that they feel unworthy and unable to conceive of a life consisting of anything else. Many victims simply internalize the values of the brothel and in time come to see themselves merely as expendable commodities to be used and then discarded. As one of my colleagues gently reminded me that morning, it is easier to take the girl out of the brothel than to take the brothel out of the girl.

In addition to this, as horrific and brutalizing as the forced commercial sexual exploitation of women and children is, some of the victims are still able to save a small amount of money, which they can sometimes send home to their impoverished families. Their rescue sometimes disrupts the only source of income for their hungry parents and siblings, and the grief, shame and anger that this arouses is often unexpected and powerful.

The situation is similar to what happens when a child is removed from a family due to sexual abuse by a parent. Leaving the child where he or she is vulnerable to further abuse is not an option. However, even when the abuse has been horrific, the child will typically still experience the trauma of being separated from a parent and will sometimes carry the unwarranted and undeserved shame and guilt as a result of believing that he or she is somehow responsible.

The young women and girls from Luton City were simply experiencing and expressing all of these emotions, and as the one responsible for their rescue, I was the logical target.

By mid-morning, the forensic dentist had arrived to conduct the age verification. In this country, as with many other developing nations, few are wealthy enough to afford official birth records, and many children either lie or simply do not know exactly how old they are. A dentist is utilized to gauge the approximate age of children by the development of their teeth and gums. The dental examinations were clearly not an exact science. Many of the girls our social workers believed were underage children were soon released along with the older girls. Ultimately only six girls were confirmed to be underage. They were established to be between twelve and fourteen years old.

During the afternoon an impromptu, informal hearing was held in the home of a local court official. He made room in his kitchen by removing some farm animals and his own children before commencing an interrogation of the alleged offenders. Much to our dismay, he also began interrogating the girls about the extent of their involvement. Again, his lack of expertise became apparent as he questioned the girls about the extent of their sexual activity. Given that their employers and perpetrators were standing in the same room, it was not surprising that the girls tried to downplay the level of their involvement. Seemingly blind to the obvious, the official criticized the girls for not being completely honest.

Watching this scene, I was nevertheless humbled by the courage of these children as they stood before this official, surrounded by numerous adult strangers, and recounted the most intimate details of the sexual activity they had been forced to engage in. They talked about their breasts being fondled, their vaginas being penetrated and their small bodies being used as toys by foreign men.

When the prosecutor was finally satisfied that there was a case to prosecute, the necessary paperwork was completed and I joined the social workers as we transported the girls by van to a remote aftercare facility operated by a local community group located several hours away. Having been up for most of the night, I found it hard to keep my eyes open as we traveled on hot, dusty roads through village after village. With the emotional roller coaster I had been on during the last twenty-four hours, I was beginning to question whether it had all been worth it.

When at last we arrived, the girls were warmly received by their hosts, and we began to say our goodbyes. Given my experience the night before, I did not expect any of the girls to acknowledge our departure. I was therefore amazed when Mahal quietly approached me and, with tears in her eyes, gave me a big hug. Looking up into my eyes, she quietly said, "Thank you, Daniel."

During my last night in Luton City I was taken by a local contact to the back streets, where those unable to work in the go-go bars sell their wares. Standing in the shadows and parking lots was a small army of girls, either too poor, too sick, too addicted or too "used" to profit the bar owners on the main strip. These women and girls had no one to protect them, no lights to illuminate their sale and no middleman or woman to witness the illicit transactions. Unable to afford the makeup, shampoo, bikini or high heels, these girls were the bottom of the barrel. Instead of the comparatively wealthy Westerners inside the bars, it was local men who made up the majority of their cruising customers.

The operative explained to me that the girls in the bars actually had it good compared to these girls, who were often raped, robbed and beaten, with little or no recourse in the law. Some disappeared altogether. He said that, in his opinion, the girls working in the bars, despite their age and the illegality of their exploitation, were the lucky ones. His comments made me aware of the complexity of the problems these girls were up against. However, in my view none of them were lucky, and no matter where they were exploited, they all deserved to be set free.

POSTSCRIPT

In order to successfully prosecute Matthew Thompson, I was asked to return to Luton City and testify on three occasions. As of this writing, eight years after our initial operation, Thompson was still running a bar, albeit under a different name, and his case was still before the courts and a verdict had not been given.

During one of my return visits, I met one of the other girls who had been rescued along with Mahal during the operation and learned more about her background. When she was thirteen, Melissa's Australian father had committed suicide and her mother had abandoned her and her two younger brothers. Desperate for money and a place to stay, she obtained a false birth certificate and went to work at the School House Bar in Luton City. She was paid a little less than $3 to wear heavy makeup and a bikini from six o'clock in the evening until three o'clock in the morning. She was further made to dance for half an hour on stage, then work the floor for a while, sitting on the knees of Korean, Japanese, German, British, American and Australian men, allowing them to grope and fondle her as they wished. If she was lucky and one of the men bought her a drink, she would make an extra $1.

The manager told all of the potential clients that Melissa was a "cherry girl," or virgin, and while many were interested, none was ready to pay the more than $900 for her virginity. "Cherry popping" is popular among the many sex tourists who traverse the globe, and Melissa knew that she would be expected to go with whoever was willing to pay the price. Thankfully, after only five nights working at the bar, the agents burst through the door as part of our operation, and Melissa was rescued. She was placed in the aftercare center with Mahal.

Three years later when I saw Melissa again, she was planning on becoming a lawyer so she could advocate on behalf of other vulnerable, abused and abandoned children.

She sent me a card, following her rescue, that I kept and referred to whenever I became discouraged: "I wish that you will never be tired of helping such many children like me. I'm so lucky for the opportunity that you gave. Thank you for all the help and support that you have given and showed me. I promise I will try my best to achieve all my goals in life, I'll reach for them, I'll try my best to succeed. I will never forget you, never."

FACTS: *Sex Tourism*

- Sex tourism is defined as traveling to a foreign country for the purpose of engaging in sexual activity.
- Sex tourism is a lucrative industry that spans the globe.
- As tourists travel to explore foreign cultures, economically developing countries have welcomed the expansion of the international tourism industry as a much-needed source of income.
- Travel agencies around the globe promote exotic sexual adventures with overseas women. Websites provide potential sex tourists with pornographic accounts written by other tourists. These websites supply information on sex establishments and prices in various destinations, including information on how to specifically procure the prostitute of your choice. Associated with the exponential rise in this industry is the growth of child sex tourism. The Internet also provides potential child sex tourists with pornographic accounts written by other child sex tourists. They supply information on sex establishments and prices in various destinations, including information on how to specifically procure child prostitutes.
- Many nations with thriving sex tourism industries are also nations that suffer from widespread poverty resulting from turbulent politics and unstable economies. Children from poor families become easy targets for procurement agents in search of young children. Governments that are struggling economically often turn a blind eye to sex tourism, thus allowing the industry to perpetuate the sexual exploitation of children.
- Gender discrimination also works in tandem with poverty. In many countries female children have fewer educational opportunities or prospects for substantial employment. The lucrative market in virgins tempts parents to sell their preadolescent daughters to brothels for high premiums. The growing demand for virgins has created a niche market.
- Sex tourism feeds the beast of sexual slavery.

8

Men

*Most men lead lives of quiet desperation
and go to the grave with the song still in them.*

Henry David Thoreau

It is easy to hate men. Men create the demand for sex trafficking, which the criminals involved in human trafficking are only too eager to supply. Without these men and their personal pursuit of pleasure, the simple fact is there would be no sex trafficking and no forced prostitution. Indeed, the entire "forced-voluntary" prostitution debate obscures the fact that the only actors within the sex industry who are actually exercising any real choice are the sex buyers. Men drive the global sex industry. Without these men, there would be no children sold into sexual slavery. Their lust and their money combine to create an unstoppable force that fuels and ultimately preys on the desperate lives of millions of women and children.

When I first started infiltrating the dark corners of the brothels and bars in the developing world, I found a number of men I wanted to kill. They included predatory sex tourists, sadistic pedophiles, cunning traffickers and greedy pimps. There were times when I just wanted to sidestep the precarious and ultimately uncertain method of gathering evidence to be used as part of a flawed and routinely corrupt criminal justice system and just shoot them there and then.

In fact, on more than one occasion, I had local police officers suggest as much to me. One high-ranking police commander even offered to supply me with a firearm and show me where to dump the bodies. He told me he had recently dealt with some Russian mafia who were known to be trafficking drugs and women into his area of responsibility. He said he took one of the gang leaders to a quiet place out of town and executed him. While I appreciated his earnest desire to assist me, I explained that the international organization I worked for would condemn such behavior.

Still, there were times at an emotional level when such an offer seemed very appealing. I recall standing in a room full of men, each trying to get the best price for the rape of the small children standing in front of them. I remember a pedophile showing me which fingers he preferred to use when penetrating his small victims. I remember numerous sleazy, fat, ugly, white men groping the slim bodies of beautiful little Asian girls who were forced to endure it all and smile at the same time. The superhero in me wanted to whip outside and change into my cape and tights before snatching the men up and carrying them off to places of fear, where they would beg for mercy.

I remember sitting in a go-go bar in Southeast Asia and talking to a young Australian man beside me. In his late twenties, good looking and with plenty of cash, he was having the time of his life. He did not bat an eyelid when a Filipina old enough to be his grandmother sat down beside him at the bar and began masturbating him. There was nothing inherently attractive about the woman, and her age and demeanor indicated that the act was one of pure desperation on her part. Once satisfied, he flicked her the equivalent of a few American dollars, whereupon she duly thanked him and departed. Without a break in the conversation, he continued to ramble on in self-absorbed chatter, the circumstances of the woman completely lost on him.

In the Dominican Republic I met an American man who worked for six months of the year in the United States as a taxi driver, saving every last dollar. This devoted sex tourist would then take his hard-earned cash and travel to a developing nation where he could live like a king on very little money. He told me that he had specifically learned Spanish so he could travel throughout Latin America and the Caribbean teaching English to young women. Yet his goal was far from altruistic. Believing me to be an apprentice in such matters, he described in great detail the necessary tools required and his ability to seduce and otherwise rape young women and girls during his "classes."

Seeing all of this through the professional eyes of an investigator was what kept me from spiraling completely out of control. When a pimp walked into a small, dark room with a little girl to sell, rather than seeing his actions through the eyes of an uncle with nieces the same age, I saw them solely as an evidence gatherer. I was therefore actually very pleased, knowing the tiny camera I was wearing was recording everything that this particular perpetrator was saying and doing, and that from an evidentiary point of view he was busted.

The other thing that kept me going was knowing I had to stay within my role. To step out of the role I was playing would certainly threaten my survival. In addition, any hope of a future intervention by the local authorities depended on me being able to gather admissible evidence that could be shown to be both reliable and fairly obtained. In short, any hope of rescuing the many victims I was offered lay in my ability to control my feelings, however angry and disgusted I felt on the inside.

There was also a certain degree of self-righteous indignation that somehow made me feel better than the men who surrounded me. It was much easier to do what I did when I saw these men as the enemy, as criminals waiting to be captured. Standing on the moral high ground, I could look down on their pathetic lives and depraved choices and join with the global community in condemning them and their behavior. Yes, it was nice to have someone to blame and it was easy to hate these men in particular. Perhaps too easy.

ENVY

I like women. I like sex. Indeed, I was attracted to many of the women I met in the bars and brothels I was frequenting. Some of the places I visited really were fantastic. The noise and the heat were often oppressive in the countries where I was working, and the bars and brothels provided a welcome air-conditioned escape from the humidity and the traffic.

Being treated like a king for a few hours was also quite wonderful. If I am honest, there were times when I was sitting at a bar with a cold drink in my hand, surrounded by gorgeous half-naked women who were attending to my every need, and I found myself thinking, *I can understand the appeal of this.* Looking at the men around me, it was clear why many of them had decided to stay around.

The more time I spent in such places, the more I realized that in many ways the men appeared to be little different than me. They were from almost every nation on earth, and they came from every profession and every class. There were builders, drivers, doctors, students, consultants, soldiers, lawyers and businessmen. Some were single; many were married. They were there in groups, and they were there alone. They saw absolutely nothing wrong in pursuing their primal desires in a way that seemed perfectly natural to them and even healthy.

It was not uncommon for some of the men to form lasting friendships with the women they met, and in keeping with their fantasy they sent them letters and returned year after year to see the same faces and pursue the same relationships, however fleeting and short-lived.

If I am honest, there were times when I even envied them. I was there to work, and they were there to play and enjoy themselves. I was there to document the very worst forms of exploitation and abuse. They seemed happily oblivious to the true circumstances surrounding the women they fraternized with. I was carrying a covert camera and was hypervigilant about my own safety and security. They could not have been more relaxed and uninhibited. And while I was friendly but guarded in all of my interactions, these men were free to enjoy all of the sensual pleasures of the flesh. And enjoy them they did.

A DIFFERENT FORM OF SLAVERY

It was part of my undercover role to make friends with such men and sometimes even to emulate their attitudes and behavior. In keeping with undercover protocol, I tried to find something about each one that I liked or could identify with, some slim link through which I could endear myself and otherwise gain their trust. And so it was that, as I really listened to their stories and shared in their lives, however briefly, I slowly began to surrender the self-righteous glasses through which I had viewed them.

I discovered that by getting to know some of these men a little deeper, learning about their life histories and their own fears and dreams, some of them were very likeable. Many of them hated what they were doing, hated their lives and hated themselves. Some of them described a series of selfish decisions that had ultimately left them addicted to a destructive cycle of abusive behavior. In this they experienced their own form of deprivation and enslavement.

Others described an otherwise boring and mundane life; their forays into the sex industry represented their only exciting escape. For a few moments in their otherwise uneventful lives these men could be the conquering hero, adored and caressed by any number of apparently willing women. Many of the men I spoke with lived for this very opportunity. In comparison, everything else seemed insignificant to them.

No amount of legislation or increase in penalties was going to stop any of them. Deep down they knew that it was a cheap substitute for adventure, an imitation of the real thing but as close as they were going to get. For any number of reasons they were aware of, and for many more they were not, they chose to pursue the lie purely and simply because they could.

Many had even created all sorts of justifications for their actions. They were providing an income to poor women and children. Without their money, they argued, people would surely go hungry. Their tourist and business dollars were providing a welcome stimulus to the local economy. But whatever their stated intentions, their underlying motives were all the same. They were all there to satisfy the same urges.

The particular "wound" that each man lived with seemed to vary in its color, shape and size. But all of them were equally eager to try to heal it by using another human being as their sexual plaything. Hungry for validation as a man, they had each embraced the idea that by using a woman or a child, they could somehow fill the void inside.

TOO EASY

During a deployment to Southeast Asia, I met a man who was selling his own teenage daughter. My fingers were quick to activate the record button on my covert camera. He described how his own illness had stripped him of his pride as well as his ability to provide for his large family. The poverty that gripped his community was endemic; some of his malnourished children had begun to suffer and slowly waste away before his eyes.

With no resources and with no one else to assist them, he had made the unfathomable decision to sacrifice one of his eldest daughters so that the other children could live. According to their culture and customs, and the perceived status of women, the entire family, including the daughter, saw this as an unfortunate yet entirely necessary act and a role that she was obligated to bear. I had little patience for any reason or excuse used to justify or normalize the abuse and exploitation of children. Neither did I for a moment endorse his decision. I imagined that if I were ever a father, I would rather die than sell my own child. Indeed I think I would rather see my own children die of starvation than see them ripped apart by the predatory lust of other men.

But that is just what I think because, thankfully, I have never had to watch a child I know go hungry. I have never had to look my hungry children in the eye and tell them as their father that I could not provide or protect them from wasting hunger pains and preventable disease.

I did not turn off my camera. The evidence gathered was duly passed on to the local authorities for them to intervene. I don't believe that there is ever any justification to sell a vulnerable child to be sexually abused and exploited, no matter what the cultural view of such circumstances. And in all my travels I am yet to find a country that will allow men to justify their criminal actions and behavior by providing an income or other necessary means of survival to desperate families and communities.

The men who choose to use others in an attempt to validate themselves need to face the consequences of their decisions. Some of them need to be imprisoned for the rest of their lives, simply for the protection of everyone else. But as I discovered, without exception the men who create the demand that fuels human trafficking are themselves slaves. They are imprisoned by the very same lust and greed they seek to profit from. They have forfeited their freedom in exchange for an insatiable hunger that is never satisfied. Hating and blaming them for their inability to break free from the invisible chains that bind them does not change anything. It is just too easy.

9

Southeast Asia

Their Names Are Lan and Milan

The Heart of Darkness is a bar similar to many others in Southeast Asia. While there is sufficient activity of a nefarious nature at
the bar, the real "heart of darkness" is located only a few hours
away in a small village on the outskirts of a northern town known
as Seri Chu. I spent several weeks in Seri Chu, and during that
time I documented more than forty girls between the ages of five
and twelve who were being sold to Western sex tourists on a daily
basis, sometimes many times a day.

Seri Chu itself is a collection of several hundred small shacks
and concrete buildings separated by dirt roads, open drains and
small wooden bridges. It was night when I first entered Seri Chu,
and it was in the company of Diego, a former member of the American Special Forces. We had been introduced through a mutual
contact, and he had agreed to assist me in infiltrating the criminal
underworld operating within the village. As soon as we entered
one of the many small restaurants on the main street, a boy of
about twelve years approached us. He asked if we wanted boys or
girls, old or young, and he promised he could take us to the very
best available.

We followed the boy along a series of dark alleyways and over wobbly pieces of wood lying precariously across the open drains and sewers that ran below. I was very conscious that with each step we moved further away from the relative safety of the main street, and I was thankful for the presence of Diego. I had spent several days with him prior to my deployment. I knew he carried a knife and was confident that he would deal swiftly and effectively with anyone posing a threat to us.

Our guide finally led us into a concrete home that was almost as dark inside as it was outside. A single light bulb dangled from a piece of wire protruding from the wall and illuminated a small room with two beds, a stool and a fan. I sat on one of the beds while Diego opted to sit on the stool. In the cramped confines of the small space, the heat was stifling. A male in his early twenties entered the room and was eager to sell us whatever we desired. Having conducted numerous military operations throughout Southeast Asia for some years, Diego took the lead in the negotiations that followed; he asked to be shown a couple of the available girls.

After only a few minutes, two girls around eleven or twelve years old entered the room and began smiling and talking with us. The male pimp explained that we could have sex with either girl for $30 each. Both girls were very beautiful, spoke some English and were well-practiced at flirting with foreigners. I was recording everything on a covert camera. Diego was aware that I had now gathered sufficient evidence to confirm the sale of children as well as the identities of some of those involved. Eager to conclude the proceedings and to extricate ourselves safely from the village, Diego looked at me and suggested we pay a deposit and leave.

EXPLOSIVES

I had read the intelligence reports on the village before my deployment and suspected that there were even younger children available. While trying to appear as casual as possible, I asked our pimp if he had anything a little younger. Diego looked at me and said incredulously, "Younger than these two?" The pimp smiled knowingly and left the room briefly before returning with two children aged six or seven and presented them to us. Diego suddenly went quiet. Despite all he had seen and experienced as a Special Forces soldier, he was unprepared to be offered a six-year-old girl for his sexual pleasure.

I then took the lead and began engaging with the children. I smiled, touched their hands, asked their names and ages, and commented on their clothing. Under the watchful eye of the pimp, the children responded with smiles, although they clearly remained nervous and more than a little afraid. To ensure that the pimp did not lose face, Diego paid him a deposit, and after promising to return later for some time with the children, we left.

As we stumbled back through the darkness heading roughly in the direction of the main street, Diego told me that he had access to some C4 explosives. Among a list of expletives, he suggested that the best way of dealing with those selling the children would be to place the C4 inside the posteriors of those responsible. While feeling the same way, I explained that the human rights organization I was working for would probably not support such a proposal, as tempting as it was.

As we walked back to our motorcycles and left the village, I was strangely excited. It was then that I realized how important my law enforcement training and experience was. Foremost in my mind was the fact that I had just captured on video clear evidence of the criminal exploitation of children, which contained images of the victims and the offenders. I had also recorded their names and knew roughly how to locate the same building again. I was in possession of a key that I hoped would soon unlock the door of freedom for the child victims involved. It was a key that I hoped would also soon turn behind those responsible for their crimes.

SEX TOURIST

Diego was unable to assist further with my mission so I recruited Bol, a motorcycle taxi driver from outside my hotel to act as my translator. He was in his mid-twenties, was single and spoke excellent English. Like most of the taxi drivers in Seri Chu, he was only too willing to act as a pimp to get a little extra money. When I explained my business objectives to him, he assured me that he knew how to get access to the youngest children available.

After double-checking my camera equipment, late one morning I met Bol outside my hotel. Straddling his motorcycle behind him, we headed back to the village. I had no backup, no support nor anyone monitoring my movements. If things went wrong, I had no escape-and-evasion plan, and Bol, who fully believed I was in his country to prey on children, was my only ally.

During the following weeks as I visited each day, I became one of the many regulars to frequent the village. On any given day I observed tourists from the United States, Canada, Europe and the United Kingdom, Australia and Japan, flocking to the village to spend their day sexually abusing, raping and otherwise exploiting the many small girls, and some boys, who lived there.

Children with pigtails and teddy bears would, as part of their daily routine, be led to small dark rooms at the back of the labyrinth of brothels and small wooden homes. There, men with money in their pockets and lust in their hearts waited. If the man was willing to pay for the child's virginity (usually sold for several hundred dollars) he could then rape the child. Otherwise he was limited to paying for the child to perform oral sex on him. Locally, the oral sex was referred to as "yum-yum." If the child's virginity had already been sold, which was generally once she turned ten, the man was permitted to have full sexual intercourse with her, referred to locally as "bom-bom."

The children I encountered during my time in the village of Seri Chu lived a life of such deprivation, depravity and abuse that most would find it difficult to comprehend. The custodians of the children beat them, tortured them, abused them and otherwise terrified them to ensure their compliance and ongoing obedience. The children were made to smile and appear as endearing as possible to each of their "clients." Complaints from the client about any reluctance or poor performance on the part of the child could mean an additional beating or some other equally cruel punishment.

I learned during my time there that some of the children had been lured to Seri Chu by relatives, promising their poor and desperate parents a better life. I interacted with many such aunts and uncles, cousins and family friends. Some of the children had been forcibly removed from their homes through trickery, deceit or outright kidnapping. And some, perhaps the most pathetic of all, were sold by their own parents. While greed and materialism played a role in many cases, other parents facing hunger or sickness chose to sacrifice one or two of their own offspring so that others in the family could survive.

During one particular transaction, I was in a room surrounded by local pimps, some only in their early teens. Standing in the middle of the group of men were two little girls about eight years old. One had her hair in pigtails, and they held hands to comfort each other. I asked the various perpetrators involved what each of the girls could do sexually and how good they were at their prescribed roles. When one of the children was asked how good she was by one of the men, she rapidly thrust her own thumb in and out of her mouth to show how good she would be at oral sex. She then raised her thumb in the air in the universal sign for "good" and smiled at me.

I began the usual process of haggling over how much each of the girls would cost when a woman suddenly entered the room and cast me a rather disapproving glance. I became embarrassed and asked if it was OK to continue to discuss the sale of the children in her presence. My concerns quickly evaporated when I was told that the woman was the mother of the girls and that her only concern was ensuring that she received a good price for their sale.

I noticed that many of the older girls, twelve and thirteen years old, had lost all life in their eyes. They appeared to be in a trance or under some kind of dark magician's spell. They moved with a slow resignation; no amount of smiling, warmth or kindness on my part could draw them out. The systematic and prolonged sexual abuse of children and young people is perhaps the very worst crime against humanity because, as I saw day after day, it strips them of their heart and soul. It murders the person but leaves their bodies alive.

I realized that the Hollywood writers of zombie horror movies were closer to the truth than they realized. However, as is so often the case with evil, the fiction fell far short of the ugly reality. These empty bodies existed in the netherworld of prostitution and in the vacuum of an indifferent world. I met them in every room of every brothel, and they all had the same look in their dark, empty eyes.

This black market within the village had operated quite openly and with relative impunity for many years. The local police chief lived near the village. Each evening his wife would enter the village and go from house to house, brothel to brothel, collecting the money that would ensure the continued cooperation of the local police.

Rumors abounded concerning even higher levels of protection that were afforded the village and those making profits from it. High-ranking government officials were said to have been seen frequenting the village and utilizing its services. The ultimate effect of such corruption meant that each of the young child victims in the village were absolutely alone with no one to protect or defend them.

CAFÉ HELL
Located beside the busiest intersection in the village was a two-story café. Along with the noise of motorcycles and the dust from

the polluted streets, patrons on the ground floor were invited to enjoy a small bowl of rice and a cool drink. Those known to the female manager, Mamasan Ngoc, were then invited upstairs to a lounge area. Here they could choose from another menu entirely made up of young prepubescent children.

After paying Ngoc, these clients took the children to one of three small rooms where they could rape the children at their leisure. Clean sheets were provided, and small fans ensured that the customers were kept cool and comfortable.

During my investigation I paid several visits to this café and was offered the very best of both menus. The intelligence gathered during this time indicated that the business had only truly begun to thrive once the United Nations workers had arrived following a civil war some twenty years earlier. Sadly some of the UN workers brought with them a guaranteed source of Western currency and perversion.

Mamasan Ngoc had been arrested only once during the twenty or so years that she ran her very profitable enterprise. She learned quickly that her business necessitated a number of contacts within the police. Once the contacts had been developed, she was largely protected from further interruption or prosecution, and she operated her business brazenly and without fear.

LAN AND MILAN

Of all the children I met during my life-changing time in the village, two little girls stood out: Lan and Milan. Only five and seven years old, these two sisters had just arrived in the village some days prior to my own arrival. When a thirteen-year-old pimp first introduced me to them, neither of them had any sexual experience and had yet to be "initiated." Their innocence and bewildered smiles captivated me, and I became more determined than ever to see them rescued.

It was only a few weeks later that I met them again, this time in their home, and in the presence of their aunt and uncle who were profiteering from their sale. I outwardly expressed satisfaction and praise when I learned that sex tourists had used both girls at least five times. I paid their relatives a deposit to secure the services of the children at a future date. And I left with fury in my heart and tears hidden behind my dark sunglasses.

At the end of my investigation, I had documented the advance sale of more than forty prepubescent children in fifteen separate locations within the village. I had obtained video footage of the offenders as well as the location of their homes and businesses. I had recorded their clandestine and illegal business operations, and had captured many of them on video as they entered into agreements and received cash in exchange for the sexual services of their respective child victims. Most importantly I had earned the trust of many of the pimps and custodians living in the village.

BOTCHED RAID

My supervisor and I disagreed about how to execute the final raid, and that became a source of frustration for me. On the appointed day we had many of the children assembled in one location, including Lan and Milan, but when the first police vehicle came roaring into the village, it served as a signal to warn all of those involved in the illicit sale of children. As some of the perpetrators scrambled to escape from the building, I grabbed one of them and began wrestling with him on the floor. The power suddenly went out and the building was plunged into darkness. Someone from outside began spraying tear gas through a crack in the wall. In the unbearable heat, the acrid air and almost complete darkness, the operation began to disintegrate into confusion and chaos. During this time many of the children fled from the building in panic.

When order was restored and the police had surrounded the building, ten children had been secured. Many of the perpetrators had successfully escaped apprehension. I desperately sought the assistance of several police officers to accompany me to the various other brothels and houses throughout the village where I knew children were being kept as sex slaves. However, they were completely ignorant of the existence of further victims or houses to be targeted. When a small team was finally assigned to assist me an hour later, it was with a growing sense of despair that we went from empty building to empty building, searching in vain for victims and perpetrators who had hastily fled elsewhere.

I was almost in tears when I arrived at the home of Lan and Milan, only to find the small house abandoned, the back door still swinging open on its hinges.

By chance I recognized two child victims and one further perpetrator as we made our way through the village. They were duly escorted back to the original target building and were loaded onto two buses, one for the victims and one for the suspects. I was thankful no one had been hurt, and I was pleased for the twelve children we had rescued. Six perpetrators had also been arrested inside the village, including Mamasan Ngoc.

Mostly, however, I was overwhelmed with frustration and despair. Of the twelve children we had secured, only six were of the original forty children that I had documented during my time in the village. I knew there were at least another thirty-four children who were hidden somewhere in the village and who would continue to be sold in sexual slavery after our departure. All the more distressing was the fact that many of these children had come to the target brothel as requested and had been so close to being rescued.

The busloads of victims and suspects left the village as part of a police convoy and traveled into Seri Chu. The suspects were duly interviewed and processed by the police while the victims were cared for and interviewed by social workers.

The following morning I went to visit the children before they were assigned to the care of the aftercare organization that had agreed to sponsor their long-term rehabilitation and care. It was an amazing experience for me to watch as they played happily with the jump ropes and soft toys provided by our social workers.

Some of the children were initially afraid when they saw me arrive, as they had only known me as the sex tourist who they had previously seen collaborating with their oppressors. Once my true identity and role were explained to them, however, one of the youngest girls disappeared briefly before she slowly approached me and shyly handed me her only possession: a small teddy bear.

POSTSCRIPT

Unbeknown to me, on the other side of the world in the United Kingdom, local police had just arrested a man for assaulting a prostitute. When searched, he was found in possession of a number of videotapes that showed him sexually abusing several very young girls somewhere in Southeast Asia. The British police were initially frustrated by their inability to charge him. Under British law they first had to prove where the offending took place, when it occurred and the identity of the victims involved. The suspect knew this and arrogantly refused to divulge any information. Amazingly, one of the officers subsequently heard about our operations in another country. Hoping that there might be a link to his case, the British authorities contacted our organization and sent us copies of the videos they had seized.

It was harrowing for me to watch in color, close up, what the systematic, pathological and cruel sexual abuse of some of the children looked like prior to their rescue. The suspect had been to the very same brothels I had documented, and his tapes covered three different visits. I recognized the same bedspreads, the same decorations and the same small faces.

After so much frustration and apparent failure, it was with some pleasure that we provided the British police with the global positioning coordinates of the brothels where he had committed his crimes, along with the names and ages of the victims. The time frame of the offenses could also be established after some immigration inquiries were completed. For one of the first times in British history, a British national was charged with sex crimes committed against children in the jurisdiction of another nation. The suspect pleaded guilty and was sentenced to a lengthy term of imprisonment.

I subsequently returned on several occasions to testify in court against the perpetrators who were apprehended during the raid. Thanks to my undercover video footage, which was very difficult to refute, all of the perpetrators were convicted. The worst offenders, including Mamasan Ngoc, were sentenced to twenty years imprisonment, the maximum under local law.

Facts: Prostitution of Children

- The commercial sexual exploitation of children has devastating consequences, including long-lasting physical and psychological trauma, disease (including HIV/AIDS), infections, drug addiction, unwanted pregnancy, malnutrition, social ostracism and death. Living conditions are typically poor, and meals are inadequate and irregular. Many children who fail to earn enough money are punished severely. Child prostitutes live in fear of sadistic acts by clients, of being raped or beaten by pimps, and of being apprehended by the police.

- While child prostitution is not legal anywhere, it is estimated that there are over 2 million children enslaved in the global commercial sex trade.

- The major demand for the sexual services of children is driven by the local domestic market. Many men believe that children are less likely to be HIV positive and that having sex with children is therefore safer. Virginity is highly prized in many cultures, and there is always a demand for young girls. The truth is, children are more susceptible to HIV and other STDs.

- Sexual offenders come from all socioeconomic backgrounds. Their distorted rationales for having sex with children are numerous. Some perpetrators rationalize their behavior on the grounds that they are helping the children financially better themselves and their families.

- Some justify their behavior by believing that children in foreign countries are less "sexually inhibited" and that their destination country does not have the same social taboos against sex with children.

- Other perpetrators sexually abuse children while abroad because they enjoy the anonymity that comes with being in a foreign land, which frees them from the moral restraints that govern behavior in their own country. And some sex tourists are fueled by racism and view the welfare of children of Third World countries as unimportant.

- Although many destination countries have passed legislation that criminalizes the sexual exploitation of children while overseas, these laws remain largely unenforced.

10

Choices

Easy money,
Lying on a bed.
Just as well they never see the hate
That's in your head!

Fantine in *Les Miserables*

One of the hardest things I had to do during any deployment was to choose one woman from among many. Inside most brothels, whenever a new client enters the building the management ensures that the women line up on cue in front of the potential customer. Depending on the size of the brothel, this ranges from as few as two or three women to as many as forty or fifty at a time. In some countries the women wear numbers on their clothing to make the selection easy and to avoid any misunderstandings due to language or custom.

Assuming the role of the predatory client was much more difficult than I had imagined. The fact is many millions of women the world over, for a multitude of reasons, choose prostitution as a viable means of survival. While some brothels were little more than slave dens, most are made up of women from a variety of circumstances and backgrounds. Often, those who are free to come and go mix and mingle with those who have the invisible hands of coercion and deception controlling their every move. In addition to acting like the sex-hungry tourist I was portraying, I had to ensure that I remained sensitive to the subtle clues and almost imperceptible signals that indicated a woman was acting under some unseen form of coercion. I would typically have a very limited time frame in which to scan the women standing before me and determine from the way they stood, the way they dressed and the look in their eyes, whether they were a victim of trafficking or not.

LIFE OR DEATH

Once I had made my choice I would usually pay whatever sum was required before being led to a private bedroom inside the establishment. It was only then that I would give an excuse as to why I was unable or unwilling to proceed with sexual intercourse. I had a long list of excuses to choose from. Sometimes I would say that men in New Zealand did not have sex until they first got to know their partner. (I was surprised at how willingly accepted this was.) Most commonly I simply explained that I had only recently broken up with my girlfriend and that I just wanted some female company. Almost without exception the women were relieved to learn that they would be paid just for talking with another lonely tourist.

It was at this point that I learned whether I had chosen correctly or not. If the woman was being enslaved and exploited in some way or was otherwise unable to leave until a debt or other demand had been met, by asking the right questions and listening carefully and compassionately to her answers I could determine whether she was a victim of trafficking. If I had chosen incorrectly and found that the woman was a willing participant who was there of her own volition, I would still try to find out as much as I could about her circumstances as well as the operation of the particular brothel I was in.

I met many amazing young women who had sacrificed their own education and dreams to provide an income for the rest of their family. While not victims of trafficking, their stories were nevertheless often just as heartbreaking.

Choosing incorrectly could also potentially place me in the company of a woman who was an ally of the criminal management. Such a woman could make extra money or earn additional favors by informing on anyone behaving suspiciously or otherwise threatening their ongoing profitability. This was especially true if organized criminal gangs were involved. Choosing the correct woman was therefore essential, not only to ensure that I did not waste time and money, but also to avoid putting my life at further risk.

During the course of the many missions I was deployed on, I had many hundreds of young, beautiful and extremely seductive women line up before me, all available for my perusal and choosing. It was only natural that I saw many women who I found extremely attractive. Add to this equation that I was already pretending to be sexually aroused and the challenge to correctly choose a victim of trafficking based on my professional ability and discernment alone was sometimes a daunting one.

The most difficult part for me was also the knowledge that in choosing one I was saying no to all the others. Choosing not to meet with and document the circumstances surrounding a particular woman inevitably meant that she would be less likely to be rescued. By not being in a position to pass on to the local authorities a photograph, her real name, date of birth, nationality and the factual details surrounding her enslavement, she was more likely to fall through the cracks of any intervention attempt. This knowledge weighed heavily upon me.

DEHUMANIZING
Having been brought up and educated in a very egalitarian country, I also found the entire selection process incredibly demeaning

and dehumanizing. It communicated very clearly to each and every woman and girl that she was only worth what someone would pay for her. Like the slave markets of old it was a most degrading and enslaving practice. To be repeatedly lined up and to go through the same process thousands and thousands of times left emotional scars that were almost visible.

I was immersed in a world where appearances were everything. The women and children I haggled over and subsequently purchased were rated solely on their appearance. I operated in a world of greed, lust and double speak, which was initially as foreign as the culture and the language. Nevertheless, my safety and the success of my mission depended on my ability to successfully read the eyes and the body language of the women as well as the criminals and corrupt officials I sought to endear myself to.

Those around me were also constantly assessing my own persona and the role I played. I had to eliminate any discrepancies between who I said I was and how I acted and behaved. Adopting the same attitudes as the sex tourists I was emulating was a matter of self-preservation. To have done anything differently would have placed me in great danger. I had to harden myself to this process. In very simple terms, to some degree at least and like every good actor, I became the person I was pretending to be.

Other investigators working undercover have described similar changes in their attitudes and behavior.

Some of us were in scenes with a lot of hookers. For a lot of us undercover cops, women [came to be seen as] second-class citizens. They are treated differently in the [criminal] scene to how I was used to treating women. Women were there to be used. [The attitude was] women didn't count the same. They were there for the guys' use . . . like drug use. Adopting the same attitudes was a matter of self-preservation when working undercover.

VIGILANCE

We are all affected and changed to some degree by the work we perform. A close friend of mine is a doctor who began training as a pathologist. He became disturbed when, as a result of the many postmortems he was performing, he began picturing the living, including those he loved, lying dead in his morgue. In a similar way my undercover work in the sex trade was beginning to change me.

Ultimately, I spent four years having naked or semi-naked women line up in front of me to be visually assessed and then chosen or discarded accordingly. As the years progressed and the number of missions increased, my collusion with this process subtly affected my attitudes. Though I hated to admit it to myself, it also inevitably and insidiously began to affect my attitude toward my own wife.

After returning home from each trip, it was taking longer and longer to relax and unwind from my heightened state of vigilance. It was also becoming increasingly more difficult to detach myself from those attitudes and ways of seeing the world that were necessary for me to survive. Perhaps most destructive was my growing inability to be completely vulnerable and open with Alice about all that I was seeing, doing and becoming.

We routinely participated in the birthday parties hosted by our friends and neighbors for their children. Alice would assist by helping to organize the food, and it was typically my job to organize the party games. It was often quite surreal to be standing in the middle of a party choosing children for various roles when only days earlier I had been choosing children of the same age to participate in a very different kind of activity on the other side of the world.

I was also unaware of how difficult it was for Alice to live alone for weeks and weeks at a time, only to be then burdened with an exhausted husband who was emotionally distant, guarded and intense. I had little understanding of how she felt when I left the home to be deployed on yet another mission. The easygoing man she had married had simply forgotten how to play and have fun. I do not know how she coped with the knowledge of what I was doing.

The choices I was making were forcing us further and further apart.

11

United States

Her Name Is Emily

On January 15, 1929, a baby boy whose dreams would change a nation was born in Atlanta, Georgia. His name was Martin Luther King Jr. King grew up in a two-story home located on Auburn Avenue in the heart of the city. Only one block away was Ebenezer Baptist Church, the base from which he would later lead a cultural revolution that would culminate in all forms of segregation being declared unconstitutional, and the liberation of America from a history of oppression and racial discrimination.

With such a rich heritage of emancipation and abolition, when I first visited the city of Atlanta I was unsure whether I would find much in the way of modern-day slavery and human trafficking. I was therefore shocked to discover that not only was slavery alive and well, but that Atlanta itself was the epicenter of such activity and indeed a trafficking hub for the entire southern United States.

Ironically, the freedoms that the civil rights movement had fought so hard to secure were now being used to recruit, enslave and oppress an entirely new generation of slaves. While the separate drinking fountains, restaurants and schools had disappeared, the same brutal system of exploitation and exclusion still thrived under a veneer of normalcy.

Inside the suburban brothels, well-camouflaged by apartment buildings and gated communities, I found girls trafficked from Mexico and Latin America. In the strip clubs, hotels and bars, I found American women living with the invisible chains of their slave masters tight around their necks. Besides the truck stops and industrial zones, I located American children selling their small bodies in the shadows and back rooms of seedy hotels and bars. But perhaps most astonishing of all, I found that the city of Atlanta was itself using its economic and political base to ensure that the commercial sexual exploitation of women and children flourished and thrived.

Atlanta is famous for its huge convention centers and mammoth sports facilities. It is no surprise then that the city can boast one of the world's busiest airports. Every year more than thirty-five million visitors flock to the region to participate in all manner of conferences, trade shows, business expos, tournaments and competitions.

Like covert terrorist cells plotting their attack, every event held in the city of Atlanta is carefully scrutinized and planned for and targeted by organized criminal groups. Coinciding with the arrival of football players, basketball fans, businessmen and music fans is the carefully choreographed deployment of a small army of sex slaves. Women and children are once again placed for sale on Atlanta's auction blocks.

DREAM CATCHERS

Posing as a foreign businessman looking to host a large corporate meeting in Atlanta, I was able to document a few of the many criminals vying for the opportunity to sell the sexual services of their slaves. My entry into this underworld was gained by befriending an erotic photographer. Kelvin Thomas was a black male who worked full time taking pictures for the many and varied porn sites, pamphlet distribution companies, prostitution rackets, and pimps selling women and children.

With large profits in mind, Kelvin eagerly invited me to accompany him on one of his jobs, and I readily agreed. We traveled together to an unused office block inside the central business district of Atlanta, where I was introduced to two men who were making money by creating an Atlanta sex guide on the Internet. These entrepreneurs eagerly showed me with great pride the many girls who were already on offer and available through their company.

A steady stream of women then began arriving for a photo shoot with Kelvin. The women came from varied backgrounds. Some were solo mothers looking for some extra cash. Others were completing a university degree and were struggling to make ends meet. All arrived with a sense of proud defiance and defensiveness in their eyes. However after only a few minutes in front of Kelvin's predatory eyes, with every flash of his camera they surrendered a little more of their dignity and their humanity. Finally, having removed all of their clothing in order to market their bodies to the highest bidder, they left with the same empty stares of vulnerable and desperate women I had witnessed the world over.

Kelvin then drove me to a secluded parking lot where he introduced me to a pimp by the name of Michael. Kelvin had told me beforehand that Michael preferred to meet at a destination of his choice so as to avoid any monitoring or surveillance by local law enforcement. Michael duly arrived in a black late-model SUV. He was a charming African American in his early thirties, well-spoken and immaculately groomed.

After exchanging pleasantries we got straight down to business. Michael said he was proud of the fact that he ran the largest amateur escort agency in Atlanta. He confidently assured me that he could access as many girls as I required and from whatever race and ethnic background I desired. When I expressed amazement and stroked his ego accordingly, Michael said that he routinely recruited girls from the shopping malls, high schools, universities and college campuses in and around Atlanta. He boasted that he could spot a girl a mile away who was down on herself. When I asked how he actually recruited the girls, he replied with a large smile, "I sell dreams."

As Michael talked, it became apparent that he was indeed a very good entrepreneur, pursuing the all-American dream. He said it did not take much effort and only a small investment on his part to gather together a group of girls. Michael said he then had each of the girls sign an employment contract, a ploy that was common among pimps. This fooled them into thinking and believing that they were somehow "legally bound" to fulfill their duties to the pimp.

As I shared a little more about my fictitious proposal, Michael explained how he could personally guarantee every woman and girl who worked for him. With little emotion and without any compunction, Michael said that he held a prescreening session with every girl. This involved him and some other men having sex with each girl to see how she performed. He then pulled out his cell phone and showed me a video of two very young African American girls engaging in oral and anal sex with different men in the same room and at the same time.

After some negotiation around the price and terms for the purchase of each of the girls, Michael agreed to meet me again the following evening to show me some of his best "products." I agreed to pay each girl $100 for her time.

As arranged, the next day Michael duly arrived at another apartment used by Kelvin for his photography business. At Michael's command, each of the girls paraded in front of me before removing their clothes and adopting provocative and seductive poses. While each of the women were of age, it was apparent from their demeanor and from the way they quickly moved when Michael spoke, that they were under his power and control.

I paid each girl and thanked her for her time. Michael was pleased with the many compliments I paid the girls, and we sealed our agreement on behalf of my imaginary clients with a hand-shake. As Michael drove away, waving from the front seat as he did so, Kelvin looked on and expressed admiration and envy for one who was so clearly making a lot of money while at the same time enjoying all the pleasures of the flesh. He had obviously not seen or identified in any way with the women sitting in the back-seat, their smiles now gone and their tired eyes staring vacantly back at us as the vehicle disappeared. This information was passed on to the local authorities.

CORRUPTION

All of the information I gathered during my time in Atlanta was given to the law enforcement authorities: federal, state and city. All were aware of the sex slavery occurring within their respective jurisdictions, and each one expressed the same frustration and sense of powerlessness at doing anything about it. They each re-counted the many meetings they had attended in order to com-municate their concerns to the Atlanta Visitors Bureau and the Atlanta Chamber of Commerce.

The law enforcement officers were united in their sentiment that while the leaders of their city were always polite and listened to evidence of the growing sexual exploitation of women and chil-dren in Atlanta, they were ultimately completely ineffectual in doing anything about it. Most disheartening of all for some of the police officers involved was the knowledge that when a young girl runs away from her home in the city of Atlanta, statistically the police have only forty-eight hours to find her before she is re-cruited into prostitution.

Those police officers tasked with combating the growth of such exploitation said that the criminal gangs involved were completely ruthless and very well-organized. Often the men who joined the gangs were more afraid of their own gang than they were of going to jail. Many of the ethnic gangs were said to be very close-knit and only targeted male customers from within their own ethnic communities, making them very difficult to infiltrate by the law enforcement community. The officers explained that at every Atlanta Convention Center event and outside every hotel, patrons would be handed information cards promoting and advertising the sexual services of those women and children enslaved in the industry.

Most alarming for me was to learn what happened during an operation set up to target some of the escort agencies involved. When it became apparent during the investigation that some of the male clients were senior members of the Atlanta city council and U.S. Senators, the operation was quickly shut down. Those officers involved were reassigned.

Many gangs used women who were trafficked into the United States and then forced to work as prostitutes to pay off the debts imposed on them. Many endured extreme forms of exploitation and abuse, and even if given the opportunity they would not speak with authorities out of complete terror. Others did not want to leave the United States and so did not complain for fear of deportation. Still others were told that if they ever agreed to testify, their families and children back in Central or South America would be murdered before their cases ever reached an American courtroom.

EMILY

I stopped to refuel my car late one evening at a gas station in an industrial area just off one of the main interstates that converge on Atlanta. A small black man materialized from the darkness and slowly approached me. He casually asked in an unconcerned manner, as if in passing, whether I wanted any "company" for the evening. When I expressed an interest, he sprang to life and the greed that lay beneath his casual veneer was exposed. He offered to connect me with whatever my heart desired and sang the praises of one particular girl who he said was young, beautiful and very "fresh."

While I paid for my gas, he made a call on his cell phone, and by the time I returned to my vehicle it had all been arranged. I would pay him $100 for the referral and I would pay the girl $300 for sex. I gave him the name of my hotel, along with my room number and cell phone number. I warned him that I would not pay him unless he delivered on his promises. He reassured me with all the charm and experience of a used car salesman before quickly vanishing into the night.

I was not back at my hotel room for long when I received a knock on my door. Standing outside was the same man I had met while pumping gas. He was in the company of a small Latino girl who was exactly as he had described her. Emily entered my room with the same forced smile, hiding a combination of dread, desperation and fear that I had seen in the eyes of so many girls in so many different countries. I duly paid the man his $100 and he left, leaving Emily to deal with me alone.

I quickly put Emily at ease by explaining that while I would pay her the agreed sum of $300, I did not want nor expect her to have sex with me. Instead I repeated my earlier ruse that I was a businessman who was bringing a number of clients to the area and that I wanted to secure the services of a number of beautiful girls who would be available to pleasure them upon their arrival. My manner as much as my story put Emily at ease, and it was only then that she began to relax.

Sixteen-year-old Emily then told me her story. She had recently traveled to the United States from Puerto Rico with her mother. However not long after their arrival, her mother died, and Emily was left alone and very vulnerable. Into this void stepped a man named Steve. Steve was a pimp and had little difficulty in providing all of the reassurance and affection Emily needed. Once he had sufficiently ensnared her in his web of deceit and manipulation, Steve put her to work in the strip clubs, truck stops and cheap hotels on the outskirts of Atlanta. She explained how she was forced to work every day, either prostituting herself to truck drivers and hotel patrons or having sex in the back rooms of a nearby strip club. She could not hide her tears as she lamented her plight and the very different dreams her mother had held for her future once they had arrived in the United States.

Having covertly recorded our conversation, I hoped that it might somehow be used by local law enforcement to intervene in some way. I then asked if I could speak with Steve directly under the guise of needing to secure additional women.

Emily duly pulled a cell phone out of her pocket and called her pimp, communicating in quick and dutiful sentences what I was proposing. After hanging up she informed me that Steve had agreed to meet with me that evening. Following Emily's directions, I drove back through the city to the same industrial area I had visited earlier. We arrived at a large, dirty, rundown and very dark apartment block, and Emily duly escorted me inside.

The interior was even worse than the outside, with bars on the windows and around doorways, an overpowering stench of urine and body odor, and anxious-looking men and women eyeing me suspiciously as they passed me in the hallway. Emily took me to the hallway outside an apartment on the seventh floor, where she asked me to wait while she disappeared inside.

I was beginning to wonder whether anyone would ever emerge, when suddenly a very large and muscular black male with a very mean look on his face stepped into the hallway. With eyes flashing and teeth clenched, he approached me quickly and, in a very threatening and intimidating manner, demanded to know what I wanted and why I was in his space.

While every part of my body screamed at me to run in the other direction, I calmly informed him that I wanted to make him some money. This stopped him in his tracks and gave him pause to reconsider his original plan of attack. I repeated the same proposal I had earlier explained to Emily in the hope that this would ensure that I left the building with my head still attached to my body and that it may have even led to further evidence against Steve.

After mulling over my suggestion, Steve agreed to help. He said he could supply even younger and more beautiful girls than Emily, and insisted that I would not be disappointed. As if to ensure that others would not thwart or compete with his new business venture, he escorted me from the building, and we agreed to meet again the following day.

Unfortunately, when Steve and I met again, he had reverted to his paranoid, angry self and was so intent on playing the angry bully that it became impossible to negotiate with him further. He was completely unable to see beyond his immediate gratification and short-term profit, nor was he willing to release Emily or any of the other girls from under his immediate control.

LAW ENFORCEMENT

Before I left Atlanta I met with several police officers responsible for the jurisdiction where Steve was operating, and I provided them with copies of all of the intelligence I had gathered to date. I hoped that they would be able and willing to intervene and use the information to prosecute Steve and place Emily in the care of a child welfare agency. However while they were grateful for the information, the officers explained that they did not have the political support of the city behind them to proactively pursue those involved in the sex industry. They went on to explain that Atlanta was an entrenched area for those advocating for the rights of women to prostitute themselves and that the scrutiny of law enforcement was generally viewed as an unwelcome and unnecessary intrusion.

STALEMATE

Unfortunately those involved in enforcing the law as it relates to the commercial sex industry, in Atlanta and in so many cities around the world, have historically focused on apprehending the women soliciting, rather than on their pimps or male clients. This is because the female prostitutes are far easier to detect, involve a lot less resources to arrest and therefore make the statistics of the relevant police commanders look all the more impressive.

The sad reality is that such an approach completely fails to identify the power imbalance involved between the women and children selling their bodies and the male patrons and pimps gaining pleasure and profit from their exploitation. By failing to effectively target those who use their power to enslave, as well as those who provide the demand for their services, the real victims of forced prostitution are lost in the stalemate that exists between those advocating for the rights of sex workers and those who are responsible for protecting the women and children who are not there by choice.

The house where Martin Luther King Jr. grew up is now a popular tourist destination, as is the church where he preached his most powerful sermons. Sadly, however, the exploitation and oppression that he railed against and challenged with his life is still very much alive in his hometown. Indeed, if the city of Atlanta has a motto, it is "Let freedom ring, and let it be rung by a sex slave."

As far as I know, Emily is still selling herself on the outskirts of the city.

FACTS: *Organized Crime*

- Organized crime comprises groups or operations run by criminals with the purpose of generating a monetary profit. The commercial sexual exploitation of women and children is a multibillion dollar industry that involves organized criminal groups in every continent and in every nation. The billions of dollars made from this criminal activity are second only to the illegal income derived from trading in weapons and drugs. This is because the bodies of women and children can be sold again and again and again.

- Organized criminal networks control large parts of the global sex industry. Many brothels simply cannot operate without the consent and protection of organized crime. The criminal gangs use their immense financial resources to purchase legitimate visas or to forge counterfeit passports.

- The criminal networks are ruthless. Violence is used to control the women and children within the industry. In some cases organized criminal syndicates from different countries will form alliances on a transnational basis to further the huge profits to be made from sex trafficking.

- A large part of their ability to operate with impunity around the world is due to corruption at the highest levels of government. Politicians often support traffickers within the sex industry because the organized criminal gangs control the balance of power.

- Many brothels are part of a larger network, and the women and girls are routinely moved to ensure new bodies are available for the clients, as well as to frustrate the identification and location of victims of trafficking. Some terrorist groups also make money to further their own political goals through the sex trafficking of women and children.

- Within the shadowy world of organized crime, the web that ensnares those victims of sex trafficking is massive, connecting thousands of otherwise legitimate businesses and people with their clandestine activities.

12

Undercover

This job is eating me alive. I can't breathe anymore.

Undercover agent in *Donnie Brasco*

Working undercover is, by its very nature, deceptive. In his book *Character and Cops*, Edwin Delattre states,

> It is the adoption of a false persona for the purpose of gathering admissible evidence against suspected criminals. . . . Undercover work requires being able to 'get inside the skin' of others. . . . [T]he more successful the undercover investigators are, the greater the trust [the] traffickers will have in them and the greater the capacity to exploit that trust.

I did not have previous experience in any undercover police work or undercover investigations. I had received very little training specific to undercover work. Prior to leaving New Zealand I met with several police officers who had successfully completed the police undercover training and had gleaned some invaluable tips from their experience and expertise. What I did not know about was the very long line of former undercover cops who had been so emotionally scarred by their work that it had devastating consequences on the rest of their lives.

Of all law enforcement assignments, undercover work puts the investigator at the most risk of corrupting his or her integrity. The undercover agent is immersed in a world of lies, distorted values and corrupt hearts. As Delattre explains:

> No matter what action is taken, there are moral costs. . . . [S]ome of those costs are paid for by the undercover agents themselves. Those who go undercover voluntarily sacrifice the opportunity for wholeness that consists of being the same person in public and in private. They engage in practices as part of a public persona that they reject in their private lives and their normal professional lives.

The inherent dangers specific to this kind of work are well-known and documented. For example, it is a common practice for many undercover investigators to begin to lose perspective and become emotionally attached to the work and to the criminals they are living with. For this reason the role of another colleague acting as a monitor or "handler" is essential. Aside from providing back up and assistance if required, it provides a vital link for the agent working under the cover of lies to the real world of truth and objectivity. It is also a means for the employer to maintain integrity by providing careful supervision and ongoing monitoring of the undercover agent.

During the later stages of an undercover deployment, danger and temptation play a greater role. After a while, undercover officers can become paranoid, feeling they have "cop" written across their foreheads. They can begin to take greater risks by conforming even further to the attitudes and behaviors of the criminals around them in an effort to ensure their cover is not blown. However, by doing so, they place themselves at even greater risk of physical, emotional and moral harm. For this reason, during and after an assignment, undercover agents are required to participate in mandatory debriefing. This is to ensure that they are processing everything in a healthy manner and are remaining in control of their emotions, choices and actions.

The personal lives of agents are invariably affected by the many days, weeks and months spent away from loved ones and the safety of home. The frequent adrenaline rushes associated with much undercover work can also become addictive, not to mention the drugs, stimulants and alcohol that can become part of their everyday life. Perhaps the greatest cost is the loss of trust, both of those within the criminal world but also of their employer, other colleagues and of personal friends and family. For all these reasons, law enforcement agencies around the world have begun to reassess "how long officers should remain undercover, what they should be told never to do and what sort of supervision they should be guaranteed."

THE GENIUS

Undercover work is "more art than science" as former investigator William Queen says: "You eventually learn the tricks of the trade on the street." So it was when I told my first lie, deceived my first criminal, documented my first case and rescued my first victim. I was enthusiastic, passionate, committed and determined to use every ounce of skill, talent, strength and wisdom I possessed to ensure the bad guys were successfully prosecuted and the victims rescued.

New Zealanders are typically self-effacing and rather unassuming. They are also generally resilient, resourceful and quick to use their initiative. Perhaps because of this, I became very good at what I did within a very short space of time. The vice president of the agency I worked for considered me one of the organization's top-drawer investigators and routinely referred to me as "the genius." He said I had the uncanny ability to bypass the careful scrutiny of the criminal groups I associated with, as well as being able to quickly identify and earn the trust of victims of sex trafficking.

I believed in the organizations I worked for, and I trusted them with my life. However some had not yet developed all of the necessary protocols and policies to properly cater to and address the specific needs of their investigative staff. While working as an investigator, I was routinely deployed overseas alone, often to work in very dangerous environments with no backup or onsite supervision or assistance. I did not have a handler at any time to monitor my progress or provide me with objective feedback. I received little formal debriefing of any kind and the services of an independent psychologist were only made available toward the end of my tenure. Even then, this was not mandatory, and most of the staff did not avail themselves of this assistance. Again, none of this was intentional. I came to realize that the organization I was working for at the time simply did not have the expertise or experience to know otherwise.

I was tasked with infiltrating the various criminal groups that made money through the trafficking of women, and this usually involved spending many hours inside a brothel or go-go bar. By their very nature these environments were designed to be extremely seductive, overtly sexual, emotionally charged and attractive to the senses. Again I was left to negotiate the dangers inherent in these moral minefields alone and with little guidance or supervision.

SEDUCTION

Traversing many hundreds of go-go bars and brothels in Southeast Asia and other parts of the world in a relatively short space of time, I met women who were very experienced in the art of seduction. It was not unusual for me to frequent as many as ten or twenty brothels or bars in one night, each establishment presenting its own unique challenges to my physical and moral integrity.

Depending on the restrictions placed on the women within each place, some were openly brazen and would confidently try to push their half-naked bodies against me. Others were more subtle and would initially sit beside me and engage in polite conversation while, all the time, moving their hands closer and closer. Some had been told to ply their customers with alcohol in an effort to lower their inhibitions and otherwise blur their moral boundaries. Those most experienced could communicate all they needed to with their eyes and their mouths from the other side of the room.

It was impossible to identify those women and girls who were either underage or who were victims of coercion and bondage without first looking at each of them. It was also impossible to remain unaffected by the visually stimulating environment I was routinely immersed in. The women were typically extremely provocative and seductive in the way they dressed and behaved. In addition to being constantly aware of my surroundings and physical safety, the greater challenge sometimes lay in remaining focused and concentrating on the mission. Obviously this was easier in some circumstances than in others.

Some within the wider community questioned the wisdom of sending men into brothels at all, whatever their motivation. As far as they were concerned such places were enemy territory and were to be avoided at all costs. I vehemently opposed such a view and maintained that if our faith in all that was good was worth anything at all, then it had to be stronger than whatever darkness and suffering it might encounter along the way.

I looked to my fellow investigators for advice on how to handle the highly charged and overtly sexual environments that were part of our job description. Their counsel was simply to "do the best you can." While this did not directly assist me in any way, it was helpful to know that they were also struggling with the same challenges and that my reactions were quite normal and wholly predictable.

We did discuss whether it would be useful to share with our wives the unique challenges we were routinely facing. We wondered whether this would somehow assist us in remaining more accountable. However we decided that whatever the benefits of honest communication, it would ultimately be unhelpful and possibly cruel to share this information with them. We agreed that the most loving thing to do was to conceal the true extent of our exposure and involvement.

We were all completely sincere in our desire to be professional investigators and effective at our work. We were also very aware of the thousands of people who were sacrificially donating to our organization so that we could be sent on our missions. Perhaps most onerously, we also carried the weight of the knowledge that we represented one of the few, sometimes the only, possible means of escape for some of the victims we encountered. To mess up their rescue and ruin their only hope of escape because of an inability to otherwise control our own sexual impulses was unfathomable and repugnant to us all.

This was another area where the organization appeared to me to be oblivious to the issues and challenges we were facing as investigators while deployed overseas. When I tried to discuss this with my supervisor, he was sympathetic on a personal level but seemed unable to fully understand my concerns. With little monitoring, oversight or counseling, we were completely at the mercy of our own emotional and mental ability to handle the unique challenges that came with our job description.

ADDICTION

I also became captivated by the work itself. I loved the excitement and the challenge of proactively thwarting the bad guys as they went about their vile business. The adrenaline that pulsed through my veins during a rescue operation was more powerful and addictive than any extreme sport or drug-induced high. The thrill of apprehending those responsible for so much suffering and the deep satisfaction that came with seeing a victim walk free from bondage and fear was exhilarating and I had never felt more alive.

It should have come as no surprise then that as time passed and I completed more missions, I started to change. This was not noticeable to me at the time, and I was only dimly aware of a growing distance between me and those around me. They could not possibly understand or relate to the things I had seen and done, and I felt increasingly unable to fully communicate with them.

Having witnessed firsthand the horror of the sex trade and knowing how relatively easy it was to do something about it, I became even more eager to return to the front lines and rescue those I knew were still enslaved. In some cases the names and the faces of the victims I had not been able to rescue began to haunt me, and I increasingly felt the burden of responsibility to go back for them.

On the one hand I knew how many desperate women and children there were crying out for deliverance and justice. On the other hand I knew how few resources and organizations there were who were proactively involved in the work of investigation and rescue. I began to feel the weight of the world on my shoulders and even came to believe that if I were not successful in my missions, then the victims concerned would never be rescued. If I did not go back for them then they would remain there forever.

I was finding it harder and harder to relax and to come down from the state of hypervigilance that my work required. These small but significant changes were the tip of an iceberg that was growing largely undetected beneath the surface of my life. And like any undetected iceberg, it was to become very dangerous.

13

Southeast Asia

Their Names Are Phi and Tan

The woman in front of me was strong and proud, but she could not hold back the tears as she recounted her recent discovery. A Canadian tourist had befriended Sawat and her family some months earlier, and in keeping with her culture and custom, she had welcomed him into her home. Sawat had appreciated his easygoing nature and the kind way he acted toward her married adult daughters and their young children.

She had received a telephone call at work earlier in the day from her husband, who said that he had become suspicious after seeing their Canadian guest using her camera while interacting with her two nieces while they lay naked on their bed mats. Both nieces were only two years old.

She immediately returned home to confront the man but found that he had gone out, leaving his bags behind. Sawat searched through his belongings and found her camera hidden in one of his bags. She also found underwear belonging to one of her nieces. Before reporting the matter to the police, she took the film from the camera and had it developed. What Sawat saw in the photographs would forever change her life.

The Canadian tourist was Kenneth Watson. He had several

false passports and was traveling under the name of Peter. What this family did not know was that Watson was a pedophile. Wanted by the Canadian police in connection with the indecent assault of several children, Mr. Watson had breached the conditions of his parole and had fled Canada. He had at least ten previous convictions for indecencies against children in both Canada and Australia. He had arrived in Lam Rai and had quickly made contact with his pedophile network. Through his connections he began finding the all-consuming target of his desires and life: small, vulnerable children.

The local tourist police acted quickly on the complaint from Sawat and apprehended Watson as he returned to collect his belongings. While they were happy to charge him with theft of the camera, they were unwilling to charge him with any offenses against the children. Their government had taken significant steps in recent years to combat the exploitation of children by Westerners. In practice, however, there was still some deference given to Western tourists and a reluctance to act against them. There are any number of reasons for this, ranging from a misplaced form of traditional Asian humility and respect, on the one hand, to blatant corruption on the other. On this occasion, for whatever reason, the police were unwilling to lay charges or investigate further.

In a desperate attempt to see some kind of justice done, a member of Sawat's family contacted the media, and the city police station was suddenly swamped with journalists and television cameras. Photographs were taken of Watson as well as his belongings, which the police kindly laid out on display for the media. Unfortunately, valuable intelligence was lost during this time as some of the items were taken by the journalists to better illustrate their stories.

Watson was allowed to speak freely with the media. He continued to protest his innocence and sought representation from the Canadian embassy. The police confirmed that they would charge

him with the theft of the camera and with various passport offenses, but that they remained unwilling to charge him with the
offenses against the children.

So it was that Sawat had contacted our local office, desperate to
see some kind of justice done on behalf of her nieces. She handed
me the photographs she had shown the police the day before. They
contained images of Phi and Tan that clearly indicated they had
been sexually abused. Along with her two nieces, there were other
images of unknown children in various suggestive poses. I conducted a brief examination of the crime scene where the photographs had been taken and drew up a scene diagram. I then took
several photographs of my own. Before leaving, I promised Sawat
that I would do all I could for her and her family.

MR. WATSON

Lam Rai is a city located in the southern part of the country and
has a population of nearly one million people. It is a popular destination for the thousands of foreign tourists who visit annually.
Surrounded by beautiful green mountains and rich in history and
culture, the people of Lam Rai are used to welcoming visitors with
traditional Asian hospitality and kindness. Sadly, it is also a popular target destination for those looking to exploit such kindness to
prey on the most vulnerable.

I contacted my interpreter, and together we traveled across
town to the city police station in an attempt to speak to Watson or
to one of the officers involved in the case. We found one police
officer present, but while he was willing to speak with me, he remained rather defensive and guarded about what was going to
happen to Mr. Watson. A short discussion ensued and I was able
to convince him to let us see Watson's property that had earlier
been shown to the media.

The police officer led me to his desk, casually pulled open a
drawer and removed a bag, which he handed to me. The contents

of the bag were an investigator's gold mine. It is common for pedophiles and other serial criminals to keep trophies from each of their victims. Watson was no different. His trophies consisted of a number of items of clothing taken from each of his victims.

He also kept an index of business cards of all the locations and contacts through whom he had been able to access children. On the reverse side of each card he had recorded the names and ages of each of his small victims: "Tai—5 years, Ban—7 years, Phan—6 years."

His cell phone contained a long list of associates and their telephone numbers. He had also kept photographs of the children he had abused, all of whom had smiled warmly for the camera. I recognized the huge value of the information to local and international law enforcement agencies, not just as intelligence but also as a means to identify and provide assistance to a multitude of previously unidentified victims.

I implored the police officer to keep the items secure, and I asked to see the station commander. The officer seemed blissfully unaware of the value of the items that lay before him and indicated that his primary concern was the theft of the camera. He communicated that the station commander would not be available until the following day. I returned to my hotel feeling very frustrated and completely powerless.

I woke up early the following morning with the same overwhelming sense of hopelessness. I was well aware that I had absolutely no legal jurisdiction to operate as a law enforcement officer. I could not demand to see Mr. Watson. Even if the local authorities granted permission, I could not compel Watson to speak with me. I felt completely out of my depth and at a loss as to how to begin to interview such an experienced criminal on foreign soil. Given the apparent indifference of the local authorities, I even began to question my own motivation and zeal, and wondered whether I was guilty of trying to impose some form of Western morality and my own values on another culture.

Nevertheless, having seen the photographic evidence, as well as the other business cards, photographs and "souvenirs" in his collection, I believed I had correctly identified Watson as the serial predator that he was. The young faces in the photographs and the names on the business cards represented a long list of destruction left in the wake of this pilgrim of narcissism. The innocence betrayed and the silent shame that was theirs cried out for justice. I felt the weight of responsibility for some of their suffering, and with it the agonizing sense of my own lack of authority and ability to do anything about it.

So, as had become my custom in similar situations of helplessness and hopelessness, I got on my knees and prayed. From somewhere deep within, the still, small voice of God gently reminded me that I acted in a moral universe where some laws were universal and that protecting and defending children from exploitation and abuse was one of them. In that knowledge I realized that while I lacked any legal authority, I already possessed all the necessary moral authority to confront and interview Watson for his crimes. In that knowledge a plan began to form in my mind. Suddenly I knew exactly what I had to do.

THE INSPIRED PLAN

I quickly shaved, discarded my usual casual attire, dressed in a sharp black suit and gelled my hair. I wanted to create the image of authority. I took the thick file notes from an unrelated case file and placed a large photograph of Watson on the top so that it was clearly visible. I made sure I had a pocket full of my own business cards, which while carrying no legal authority, nevertheless displayed an impressive golden seal. Last, I arranged for another colleague to accompany me to the police station, also wearing a black suit and carrying a covert camera inside his bag to record our proposed interview.

We arrived at the station just as prisoner visiting hour commenced. Along with a number of locals, we were granted access by the jailer to the cell block in the basement of the station. We followed a junior officer as he led us downstairs to the main holding room. A wall of bars separated us from the prisoners, and we were instructed not to touch the prisoners or stand too close to the bars. As some of the locals greeted their family members and friends, my interpreter asked to speak to Mr. Watson. After a few minutes, Kenneth Watson was escorted to the front of the bars, where we could speak with him freely. He quickly appraised us and seemed intrigued but not in any way intimidated by our presence.

In his fifties, Watson was Caucasian, overweight and balding. Handing him my business card and making sure he could see the large file with his photograph on it, I confidently introduced myself and my colleague. Watson seemed surprised by our visit, but I indicated both verbally and nonverbally that we knew all about him.

During the thirty-minute conversation that followed and by using a range of interview techniques that I had learned as a rookie detective, Watson eventually confessed to sexually violating one of the two-year-old girls and indecently assaulting the other. He also admitted an indecent assault on a previously unknown seven-year-old boy.

Watson was about to be granted bail the following day by the local police. Having obtained our confession, we quickly left the station and returned to our office. The recorded confessions were then translated into the local language and appropriate subtitles were placed on the videotape. Early the following morning we made an appointment to meet with the district police commander. Having reviewed the videotape and the confession, he directed that Watson be kept in custody and that he be charged with the sexual assault of the two small girls.

In the days that followed I received a telephone call from a freelance journalist who had been following the case along with the rest of the local media. She said she had been to speak with Watson in prison and had been horrified to find children in the cell with him. She had learned of our involvement from Sawat. She asked me to investigate further and to do all I could to stop it. Recalling my own days as a junior police officer responsible for prisoners in police custody, I found it hard to believe that anyone would allow a suspected pedophile currently incarcerated and facing sexual assault charges to have access to other children.

So it was with some skepticism that I returned with a translator to the city police station and was again granted access to the cells. To my dismay, I found Watson in his shower with a young boy no more than eight years old. Due to the absence of a social welfare institution to care for the dependents of prisoners, there were a number of entire families imprisoned in the jail block.

Seeing me, Watson quickly got dressed and, with a guilty yet defiant look on his face, maintained that he had done nothing wrong. He told me that he loved the bodies of children because they were "perfect" and "unblemished," and he communicated no remorse for his insatiable lust.

The translator chastised the prison guard on duty for allowing the child into Watson's cell. The child was quickly removed and returned to a nearby cell where his parents were both incarcerated. The parents listened intently to the translator as he described the nature of the charges against Watson, and as he implored them to protect their children accordingly.

Given the economic disparity between Watson and the others who shared his jail, we ultimately left the station unsure whether a bribe or monetary payment of some kind might still facilitate further access to the children around him.

Kenneth Watson subsequently pleaded guilty to performing an indecent act on the two children and was sentenced to a period of two years imprisonment in a local jail. I subsequently liaised with the Canadian embassy to ensure that Watson would be extradited back to Canada to face further charges upon his release.

One of the most powerful moments for me throughout my short human rights career was meeting one of the mothers of the two small girls. Asian people are generally emotionally restrained. Despite her best efforts, however, the mother could not hold back her tears as she expressed her thanks for ensuring that justice was done on behalf of her child. It was incredibly exhilarating to know that my skills as a detective were used by God to bring justice to a poor family on the other side of the world.

FACTS: *Pedophiles*

- Pedophilia is the primary or exclusive sexual attraction of adults to prepubescent children. A person with this attraction is defined as a pedophile. A large number of pedophiles are respected members of society, working in positions of responsibility and trust.

- The pedophile is driven by an obsessive desire to have a sexual relationship with a child. Pedophiles are predatory. Many hours of planning and manipulation will typically be necessary for the pedophile to secure his desired goal.

- There are pedophile clubs and organizations in most Western countries. They generally operate in a highly secretive and very organized fashion. Increasing numbers of pedophiles have purchased bars, hotels, guesthouses and resorts throughout the developing world. These are run and frequented by other pedophiles or people sympathetic to their needs. Pedophiles have their own survival manuals and travel guides, which are published specifically to help their members avoid detection and prosecution in the countries they visit.

- As well as using the Internet to prey on children online, it has also facilitated the discreet sharing of information and online intelligence between pedophile networks.

- Pedophiles are virtually unrecognizable, and hence the belief by most experts is that pedophiles can be anyone.

14

Church

I can't stand your religious meetings.
I'm fed up with your conferences and conventions.
I want nothing to do with your religion projects,
Your pretentious slogans and goals.
I'm sick of your fund-raising schemes,
your public relations and image making.
I've had all I can take of your noisy ego-music. . . .
Do you know what I want?
I want justice.

Amos 5:21-24 The Message

Erwin McManus writes: "There may not be a more dangerous weapon for violence and oppression than religion." However, wherever there is authentic faith expressed through genuine compassion, the church can be the most powerful source of hope and courage to victims of trafficking.

Many trafficked women and children have internalized their shame and see themselves as worthless and somehow deserving of their degrading abuse and exploitation. They hunger to know that they have value, that they do matter to someone and that there is a hope and a future for them. Genuine compassion rooted in the knowledge that they are loved by their Maker offers a way forward.

The oppression inherent in human trafficking often includes an overt negative spiritual component. For example in the Caribbean, I found that it is common practice for traffickers to place a voodoo curse on the women. The women are told that the curse would come into effect should they ever talk to the authorities or testify in court. For those involved, this is a very real and very powerful form of spiritual enslavement, one that can only be broken by placing their trust in a spiritual power greater than the black magic. Field workers from the International Organization for Migration who worked with many of these women told me that only after their conversion to Christ would the victims agree to talk about their experiences.

With a mission to fearlessly expose evil and rescue those oppressed and enslaved, the church has been called to be the perfect abolitionist. Indeed the church has a rich history of courageous men and women who have selflessly rescued and restored the exploited women and children of their day.

During the first centuries of the church, baby girls were considered by many to be a liability. Female infanticide was common, and pagan society not only approved of the practice but also encouraged it. It was permitted by law to simply leave them outside the city on the garbage dumps to die. But the early church refused to accept their culture's assessment of baby girls and went outside the city to find and rescue them.

Since then the church has played an integral part in setting captives free from slavery and injustice. With small groups of believers, missionaries, relief and development organizations, priests, and committed disciples operating in almost every corner of the world, church and parachurch organizations are often the only ones with the necessary language ability, cultural understanding and local knowledge to document the various forms of oppression and injustice occurring within their own communities.

MY EXPERIENCE

During my time investigating human trafficking, the most challenging thing for me was when I found the church to be absent from the fight. At a time when there are more people in slavery than at any other time in history, tragically I found the church in many countries to be largely silent or completely unaware of the slavery around them.

On any given Sunday I often sought out a place of worship near the area where I was operating. Indeed, I had found that such times of stillness, surrender and reflection were essential to my ongoing effectiveness. However, what I often saw was a church that had allowed itself to be seduced, entertained and enslaved by a form of worship inherited from the West: the focus was more on the feelings and desires of those present than on a suffering world that was crying out for rescue. The goal was typically on gaining victory over personal sin, and there was little apparent understanding of the whole gospel as it applied to the rest of a creation groaning under the weight of injustice and evil.

In both the developing and the developed world I was struck by the sometimes ornate and overtly expensive buildings into which the faithful filed on any given Sunday morning. Sitting in the air-conditioned complex discussing Christian theology as it applied to relationships, marriage, family and employment practices was all very nice. In the light of what I had seen during the week, however, such debate and discourse seemed empty and devoid of any authenticity because there was no involvement on behalf of those most enslaved and oppressed within their own communities. Indeed, I routinely found that I was more uncomfortable inside such a church than I was inside a brothel. At least inside the brothel there was no pretense.

The church has always sought to communicate to a hurting world that God is a rescuer who can save them. Our message has little credibility while we remain afraid, indifferent and inactive in the face of human slavery occurring in our own backyard.

Sadly, as I reflected on this, I realized that the fear that I carried into the very first brothel I visited was a fear I learned in the church. It is there we learn to fear our sinful nature. We learn to be suspicious of the world, and we fear those who may threaten or harm us or our families. We tend to either fear evil or trivialize it. And perhaps most daunting for the Western church, we fear failure. In a culture governed by management ideals and pragmatic strategies for success, a willingness to live faithfully before God no matter what the circumstances, costs or outcomes is especially challenging.

CRISIS OF FAITH

When I started out on this adventure of righteousness and justice, I believed what I had been taught in church; namely, if I obeyed God, he would do his part by showing up and doing great things through me. I had, after all, sold everything I owned, traveled halfway around the world away from my loved ones, and was putting myself in great danger to do his will. Given these sacrifices, I believed that God would take care of my family and me, and that he would successfully use me to bring freedom to the women and children imprisoned in commercial sexual exploitation.

I humbled myself before God, I prayed and faithfully did everything I could to intervene. After that, I expected to see results! I had come to see God as the perfect superhero, and like every superhero, I expected him to come through for me and especially for those held in slavery crying out for freedom.

I had a crisis of faith when, for whatever reason, my missions failed or were aborted. I believed in a God who listened and answered prayer, and who promised to give me whatever I asked for in his name. I had no doubt that rescuing victims of slavery was his will and that he wanted them to find freedom, restoration and redemption more than I did. So when things did not go according to plan, I vented my frustration and anger toward God.

Given the extremely dangerous and seductive environments I was working in, I asked for and expected God to give me the supernatural ability to successfully negotiate any and every temptation, and to overcome my sinful nature on every occasion. However, in moments when my own flesh betrayed me and when the traitor within gave way to temptation and selfish lust, the sense of moral failure I experienced was overwhelming and utterly devastating.

In wrestling with my disappointment, I found strength from the words of pastor Erwin McManus. He states that Western Christians in particular have a superficial understanding of what it means to follow Christ. "All of us think . . . when we live by faith, we don't die by the sword. When we live by faith, every battle is won and every enemy conquered. . . . [But God] has far deeper and more profound work to do in and through us." He argues that if we believe in God only because of the outcomes he guarantees, our faith is not based on love and trust but on what we think God owes us. "We've been taught that every story Jesus writes with our lives ends with 'and they lived happily ever after.' . . . The civilized view of Jesus is that He always comes through for us. Like Superman, He always shows up just in time."

But life is unfair. Evil things happen to good people. In our life on earth, sometimes the bad guys do win. And those who have experienced such suffering are right to scorn the Hollywood fairy-tales masquerading as Christian faith.

DANGEROUS COURAGE

In the face of all this fear the biblical imperative is to act boldly and with courage when staring evil in the eye. When the Israelites were doubting themselves in the light of their past sin and failure, God said,

> Do not fear, for I am with you;
>   do not be dismayed, for I am your God.

> I will strengthen you and help you;
>> I will uphold you with my righteous right hand. (Isaiah
>> 41:10)

In the face of hostile enemies, God instructed Joshua, "Have I not commanded you? Be strong and courageous. Do not be terrified; do not be discouraged for the LORD your God will be with you wherever you go" (Joshua 1:9). In the face of evil men of criminal intent, Jesus warned his disciples, "Do not be afraid of those who kill the body and after that can do no more" (Luke 12:4).

Writing from inside a prison where he had been thrown because of his faith, Paul exhorted the disciples of Philippi, saying, "I eagerly expect and hope that I will in no way be ashamed, but will have sufficient courage so that now as always Christ will be exalted in my body, whether by life or death. For to me to live is Christ and to die is gain" (Philippians 1:20-21). In the face of the spirit of the antichrist, John exhorted his brothers and sisters by reminding them "greater is He who is in you than he who is in the world" (1 John 4:4 NASB). Catching but a glimpse of the wild abandon common among those who have overcome their fear of evil will make us shout and celebrate with the psalmist,

> The LORD is my light and my salvation—
>> whom shall I fear?
> The LORD is the stronghold of my life—
>> of whom shall I be afraid? (Psalm 27:1)

If we turn our hearts toward God and fear only him, we are no longer bound by all the other fears that would hold us captive. Fear of our sinful nature, fear of the world, fear of evil and our fear of failure can only be conquered when we fear God alone. McManus concludes: "We resist love to avoid pain and squelch our dreams out of fear of failure. For the Spirit of God to unleash dreams and visions within our souls, we must become free to risk and to fail."

It is time the church was honest about the fact that Jesus did not come to make us successful and to save us from suffering. He asks the same question of those on this mission that he has always asked: in the face of slavery, suicide, disease, disaster, divorce and death, will you still love me? Though this life I have called you to live may slay you, will you trust me? It is this simple yet thoroughly subversive trust that makes us so dangerous to the forces of evil and oppression. Suddenly we are no longer bound by a defensive attitude but by a proactive stance that takes a risk and goes on the offensive.

The worship lyrics of most modern churches are often inserted into a PowerPoint image depicting the beauty of nature or the majesty of the universe. How would our worship change if we used images of imprisoned slaves instead? What would happen if we stopped asking to see God in heaven and instead asked to see him in the eyes of prostituted children? What would happen if in the face of the very worst forms of depravity and evil in the world Christians walked in the knowledge that they are the dangerous ones and the ones to be feared?

The successful rescues and the devastating failures associated with my work were stirring in me a deep desire to see the church of Christ around the world act with courage in the knowledge that light is indeed stronger than any darkness.

15

Southeast Asia

Her Name Is Sua

Suspicious guards wearing two-way radios and earpieces watched me carefully as I advanced toward them in the darkness. Giving the casual appearance of a relaxed tourist, I asked if they had any girls available inside. The first guard eyed me carefully before telling me there were no girls available. The second man scolded him before giving me a quick smile and barking something into his microphone. Behind him the large steel door slowly opened and he waved me past before closing and locking the door behind me.

I was in Kedang Tebal, the capital city of Pengor, in the western part of the country. With nearly two million people in the larger metropolitan area, Kedang Tebal is one of the largest metropolitan areas in the country. It is a very popular destination, with more than ten million tourists visiting each year. One of the reasons for this is that Kedang Tebal has a thriving sex industry, and thousands of Western and Asian men flock to the area because the laws are less restrictive and the sex is cheap.

We had received a complaint from the family of a Thai woman who had been trafficked by a man named Sonny to a brothel in Kedang Tebal. The woman had somehow managed to escape and return to Thailand. However, she reported that there were still a large number of Thai women and young girls being held against their will by the same criminals who had enslaved her. She was able to supply the names of three brothels, all in close proximity to each other where the victims were being held.

Two Thai investigators were dispatched to the three target brothels, but they were either not allowed access or were monitored so closely by the heavy security that their visits were ineffective. I was therefore deployed to see whether I could infiltrate what appeared to be a well-organized and very lucrative criminal enterprise.

Upon my arrival I was able to debrief the two Thai staff and found out that the brothels in Pengor were unlike anything I had encountered. They noted that a sophisticated network of informants, lookouts, guards and security staff provided constant protection for the brothels concerned. Each brothel had guards on the perimeter, guards on the doors and guards inside each building. They were each equipped with two-way radios and were in constant communication with each other. Each visitor was screened before being allowed inside, and in the case of the Thai investigators, both had been physically searched upon entry.

The trafficker known only as Sonny delivered girls to a number of the brothels in the area, and the managers and owners of each brothel constantly moved the girls to further thwart the possibility of any outside intervention. The brothels themselves were huge factory-style premises: concrete two-story buildings that communicated little of what was occurring inside.

Our intelligence suggested that the owners were very well connected and that senior local government officials were regular beneficiaries of the services offered. The brothels in turn were run by a Mafia-style hierarchy with links to local hotels, businesses and tour companies. Such an environment allowed the organized criminal networks to flourish; the sex-trafficking market provided a lucrative return for all involved. This country's geographical proximity to the impoverished nations of Cambodia, Laos, Vietnam and Myanmar provided these well-organized traffickers with a ready source of "raw materials."

The presence of organized crime meant that the targets would be more difficult to infiltrate, the perpetrators more sophisticated in their methods and the anticipated rates of return for their investments high. This was a multimillion-dollar business enterprise. It also meant a much greater risk to anyone trying to infiltrate and document their criminal dealings.

Unfortunately, my two Asian colleagues had to return to their home country unexpectedly, and I was left to proceed with the investigation alone. I knew that it was not a good practice to operate without any backup in a foreign country with no language ability and little time to acclimate myself to the local culture and geography. However, we had received significant and specific intelligence suggesting that several of the key criminals involved in the trafficking of hundreds of girls were at one of the three brothels to be targeted. Relatives of some of the still-missing captives had pleaded with the organization to act on their behalf, desperate to see their daughters, granddaughters and sisters alive again.

Most of the girls had traveled south from China, Laos, Myanmar and Thailand with the promise of well-paid employment as waitresses, domestic servants, nannies and receptionists. When they arrived, they found themselves ensnared in a web of deception and corruption, operated by men and women only too willing to do whatever was necessary to turn the vulnerability of these young women into their own profit. They were systematically raped and imprisoned. They were threatened with violence should they try to escape, and they were told that if they did flee before their imposed debts were repaid, their families would be harmed and their younger sisters or brothers would be taken in their place.

With the weight of this knowledge on my mind, I decided to

proceed with the operation. After conducting some initial surveillance, I booked a hotel nearest to the first target and began to mingle with some of the other guests and male staff. When evening came and I discreetly inquired about local brothels, I was duly directed to the target in question and was given additional tips on how to get the best deal available.

FACTORIES OF SLAVERY

So it was that I found myself entering a very large two-story brothel, which, in contrast to the nondescript darkness outside, had a brightly lit and expensively decorated interior. There were an additional three security guards relaxing near an open bar area, all equipped with the same two-way radios. One of them came forward and greeted me before asking me to follow him up a staircase to the left of the bar. He asked me where I was from, to which I replied, "New Zealand."

As we reached the top of the stairs he walked quickly past an open lounge area before turning down a long corridor. As I followed him past the lounge, I saw that there were ten to twenty girls sitting on a long couch. They were all Asian, in their late teens and early twenties, wearing short skirts, skimpy tank tops and heavy makeup. Their eyes told me all I needed to know about the place. I made brief eye contact with one girl who stared straight through me, a sad and detached look on her face.

The guard ushered me into one of the many small rooms on either side of the long corridor. The tiny room had two small couches separated by a small coffee table. The lighting was low and a small speaker pumped music into the room from an outside source. Pausing only to ask what I would like to drink, he shut the door behind him, leaving me alone in the room before disappearing. A short time later, he returned with some beer and three Asian girls in their late teens. Each girl wore a tight shirt displaying her breasts and a very short skirt that barely covered her backside. I ordered drinks for the three girls as well and the guard left.

Away from the presence of the guards, the girls noticeably relaxed and engaged in lighthearted banter with me. For the next thirty minutes we talked and exchanged stories. I learned that all three girls were from Thailand, that all three had been deceived into coming to the brothel under the promises of another job. All three were desperate to escape and return to their homes and their families. I also learned that nearly one hundred girls in the brothel were being held prisoner. This casual conversation in a small cubicle on the second floor of a brothel in Kedang Tebal was about to spark one of the largest antitrafficking operations this country had ever seen.

SUA

I met Sua in the Yamagen brothel. I arrived by taxi at the rear entrance of the brothel just as a group of Chinese men was also arriving. A guard from behind a large steel door visually examined us before the door opened and we all filed inside. Once inside it became apparent that the security staff had assumed I was with the Chinese men who had unwittingly assisted me in gaining entry. I was ushered into a small room to wait by myself. A large, powerfully built man with a shaved head then appeared and introduced himself as the manager. He was intimidating in appearance but was otherwise friendly and accommodating. He spoke a little English. His name was Ghani.

I asked for a drink and then asked if he had any girls who spoke English. Ghani said he did, and a short time later he returned with Sua, a Thai girl who appeared to be in her early twenties. She spoke good English, having studied it at high school. Sua was very polite and did not have the overly familiar traits of a girl who had worked in the sex industry for some time. Ghani and some of the other guards initially checked on us, but because we were talking in English, they left us alone.

Sua communicated that she was from Bangkok and had only been at the Yamagen for two months. She said she had come because a friend had told her that she could get a job at a car dealership. However, upon Sua's arrival in Kedang Tebal, her passport was taken and she was told she would have to work at the brothel for at least six months or until she had paid off the debt they had imposed on her before she could leave. She said that she lived at a house near the brothel with seventeen other girls who also worked at the brothel. She confirmed that they were locked inside and were not free to leave.

Sua indicated a willingness to spend the evening with me, so I spoke with Ghani who confirmed it would cost me approximately $100. I paid him the required amount, recording the purchase on my hidden camera. It became apparent that Sua was allowed to leave the premises in the company of a client. Ghani took down the details of my hotel and my room number, and as an extra privilege he told me that Sua could stay with me until 11 a.m. the following morning. Two security staff were assigned to accompany us, and we began walking toward the rear exit.

Sua then stopped to talk to another solidly built man seated at the bar. He appeared to be of Chinese descent and had a tanned complexion and short, tidy, black hair. When he looked at me, I stepped forward to introduce myself and said I was from New Zealand. The man's eyes lit up and he said his name was Sonny. I had finally come face to face with the man responsible for the trafficking of so many.

Sua explained that Sonny was her boss. I told him I liked Sua very much. Sonny said I should return the following day at 3 p.m. when the bar opened and have a drink. I thanked him for the invitation and turned to leave. As I did so, I was careful to capture his face on my covert camera.

The two security guards accompanied Sua and me back to my hotel and even walked beside her to my hotel room. They duly noted the room number and left, leaving Sua and me alone.

SECURITY EVERYWHERE

Sua noticeably relaxed after the guards departed. Once settled in our own room, Sua explained that she was twenty-five years old. She said she had married a soldier who was on holiday in Thailand and that they had a son together. Her husband had then been sent into active service with his regiment and had sadly been killed. In search of a well-paying job, Sua had asked her mother and father to care for her son while she traveled south to secure employment. Upon arrival in the city, the car dealer she had expected to work for turned out to be the manager of several brothels. Sua was raped and had her passport forcibly taken from her. She was then imprisoned before being told that what she would be selling was her own body.

With resignation and hopelessness, she went on to say that she had only recently learned that her mother had taken her son on holiday to the island of Phuket, where on December 26, 2004, both had been killed in the giant tsunami. When she told the manager about her tragedy, he was unmoved and only confirmed that it changed nothing as far as he was concerned.

When I asked Sua about the possibility of trying to escape, she pointed to the constant surveillance that she and the other girls were under. "Always, everywhere, security," she said. Sua explained: those she worked for were brutal men who frequently used violence to control the girls. She also said that she was constantly tired, starting work every day at 4 p.m. and working through the night until daybreak the following day. She said sometimes she had more than twenty clients during that time, and that by the time she and the other girls had finished their shift they were exhausted.

I took the risk of asking her some overt questions about the way the brothel operated. Despite her misgivings, she provided some information about the conditions where the girls lived and when they were transferred to the brothel each evening. Sua said there were a number of secret passages and hiding places within the brothel where the girls would be hidden if the police attempted a raid. She added that many of the local police officers were regular customers and that a raid was very unlikely. She recounted stories of the management receiving a tipoff whenever a raid was about to occur. Once all the girls were safely secreted, the local police officers executed their "raid" and, as anticipated, found nothing. Once they had completed their duty, these same officers were allowed back into the brothel to spend time with the girl of their choice.

Sua said even if she did try to run away, she had nowhere to go and no one to run to for help. She had been told that if she went to the police, they would arrest and hold her in jail for being an illegal alien. She did not even fully understand where she was being held within the city; due to her detention she did not know the city at all.

After talking for some time Sua tried to initiate sex with me and was initially confused when I declined her offer. In keeping with my cover story, I told her that I had only just broken up with my girlfriend and that I felt emotionally unable to participate. I expressed a needy desire to just be close to someone, and she accepted this.

We got into bed together, and Sua gave me a hug before quickly falling asleep, relieved on this occasion that she did not have to "earn" her rest. Lying in bed beside an attractive, half-naked twenty-five-year-old prostitute, I was thankful not to have succumbed to temptation. I was equally very conscious of the huge value of the information that Sua had provided and was optimistic that something could be done for her and all of the girls enslaved with her.

The next morning while Sua was in the shower I discreetly contacted a colleague who had arrived in the city to assist me. I asked him to drive to my hotel before the prearranged pickup time. I wanted him to try to follow the guards who were driving Sua back to the house near the brothel where she and the others were being held. With rush-hour traffic, it was going to be a challenge—even more so given that my colleague was a lawyer who had no experience in surveillance and did not know the local geography at all. Following breakfast, Sua was picked up by the security staff as arranged, and in order to further the ruse, I gave her a long hug in their presence. I genuinely felt considerable compassion for her. Knowing what Sua was returning to also made it difficult to let her go. As we walked together down to the parking lot, and as she was escorted to a waiting vehicle, I quickly passed on the description of the vehicle via cell phone. Unfortunately my colleague quickly lost his quarry at the first traffic lights, and Sua disappeared into the congested motorways.

I spent the day typing up my daily report to send to my colleagues in New York, hoping that some of the planning and preparation for a possible intervention could get underway. Later that evening I returned to the Yamagen brothel and again asked for Sua. I was told she was with a client. While I waited, I bought Ghani some beer and we talked about his lavish home in the countryside. He invited me to travel there with him during my next visit and to enjoy his swimming pool and hospitality. Given the relationship I had quickly developed with him, I inquired about the availability of virgin girls.

Ghani went to get Sonny, who was more than willing to assist. He said he had four virgin girls available for purchase and asked if I wanted to view them. He said he kept them at an offsite location for security reasons. I was already operating alone, and I had no way of contacting anyone to let them know where I was if I agreed to go with Sonny. As tempting as it was to document even more victims, I opted to stay with Sua and concentrate on the target in hand.

When Sua eventually arrived, she was pleased to see me but was clearly tired, having already been with four clients prior to my arrival. I indicated that I wanted to spend time with her again, and this time Ghani explained that I could pay for a "short time" encounter with her in an adjacent building. I agreed to do so and Ghani left. Sua's demeanor was visibly different from when I had last seen her; she was fearful and unwilling to speak. She quickly begged me in a whispered voice not to discuss her leaving the Yamagen again, and she put her finger to her lips to indicate that there were people listening. I indicated that I understood and followed her to a rear door at the back of the building.

A guard standing beside the door spoke into his two-way radio before quickly giving a signal to Sua as he opened the door. Sua took me by the hand and walked quickly down a dark alleyway. Along the dimly lit side streets I could just make out the forms of more security staff watching us as we made our way to another steel door located in the side of a concrete wall. Upon arrival, the door opened instantly, and we were again ushered inside.

The guard smiled at me as we entered before quickly locking the steel door behind us. After uplifting two condoms and a towel from a large basket, I followed Sua down a long hallway. On either side of the hallway, small doors opened to small dimly lit bedrooms. The sounds of sexual activity could be heard coming from some of the rooms, a reminder to me to talk quietly with Sua lest someone overhear or monitor our conversation.

WHISPERS OF FEAR

When we were alone in one of the small cubicles provided, Sua continued to whisper. Now that she was back within the confines of the brothel, Sua clearly regretted telling me so much information and was terrified that I might try to help her escape in some way. She explained that from her point of view it was impossible to escape and that I would only be endangering her by trying to get her out. She was adamant that she would just continue to pay off her debt until she was allowed to go free. Sua said that of the

$100 that I had paid for her the previous night, she kept only $40 while the $60 went to pay off her arbitrarily imposed "debt." When I asked about trying to identify where she was being kept during the day, Sua begged me not to discuss it any further. I duly agreed, and we sat in silence as Sua quietly gave me a shoulder massage.

When our allotted thirty minutes were up, I lightheartedly picked up the two condoms and said that I would take them with me to remember her by. From an evidential point of view I also considered this an important thing to do in that the condoms were evidence of sexual activity occurring at the location. I was surprised at the extreme reaction Sua had to my comment. With great dignity and spirit, she said she did not want to be remembered by anyone because of two unused condoms and that if I cared anything for her at all, I would give them back to her. As I handed them back to her, she looked at me again with vulnerable confusion and gently asked why I cared about her at all.

Sua escorted me back through the gauntlet of guards and security to the main building. Ghani saw me and, for some reason, seemed eager to quickly escort me out of the building. Fearing that our conversation had somehow been monitored or overheard, I tried to appear calm as the tension and adrenaline suddenly surged through my system. Waving goodbye to Sua, I followed Ghani to the rear door where he stood aside to let me pass. As I walked out into the warm air, every dark shadow and every passing vehicle presented a major threat in my mind, and by the time I made it back to my hotel, I was completely drained but very relieved.

I saw Sua one last time the following evening when I returned to the Yamagen to say goodbye to Ghani and Sonny. I hoped that I would be involved in any subsequent intervention on behalf of the authorities, and I wanted to ensure that I remained on good terms with them both. They asked me to bring them both gifts when I next returned, and I said I would.

Sua then approached me and handed me a silver ring. She quietly said that she had asked one of the other girls who was allowed to leave the house to buy it for her that day in the market. She asked me to wear it to remember her. The brothel manager and guards looked on as I hugged her warmly and left. Placing her ring on my finger, I quietly prayed that Sua and her friends would soon be free.

POLICE RAID

The information provided by Sua and the other girls inside the three brothels, along with photographs of the victims and perpetrators, plans of the internal layout, and details of the security and surrounding environs were all compiled in an extensive and very detailed report. In an effort to sidestep the corruption, this information was forwarded to some of the highest-ranking officers in the area. Assurances were given that the rescued girls would be treated as victims and not charged with immigration violations. A plan of action was proposed that would net the perpetrators responsible.

The authorities ultimately declined our offer of assistance with the planning and execution of a raid. They also declined to include me as part of any "buy-bust" sting operation.

Early one morning a few days later, police officers from another city traveled west to Kedang Tebal and executed raids on the three brothels identified. Unfortunately, information was still somehow leaked to the local authorities and found its way back to the owners and managers of the brothels. When the police raided the premises, few of the trafficked girls were present.

Thankfully, one of our Thai staff had been able to initiate contact with some of the Thai girls who had access to a cell phone, and they were able to communicate the location of the safe houses where they were being hidden. With this information the authorities were able to successfully locate and secure seventy-nine victims of sex trafficking, one of the largest operations of its kind to date.

In the months that followed, the girls were interviewed and processed. The embassies of five nations located throughout Southeast Asia were all intimately involved with the repatriation of their citizens. With the exception of a small number of girls from the Golden Triangle whose citizenship proved very difficult to establish, all were successfully repatriated within a relatively short period of time.

Despite the testimony of all of the women and girls rescued, as well as the detailed offender information and photographs provided to the government, to date none of the perpetrators associated to this case has been arrested or prosecuted. None of the victims I had interacted with, including Sua, were rescued; their whereabouts remain unknown.

I was thrilled that so many had been rescued, but yet again I was unable to celebrate knowing how many we had missed. I was especially upset that Sua had not been located. Given that some of the information we had supplied to the authorities later found its way into the hands of organized crime, to this day I remain haunted by what may have happened to Sua and to the other girls I spoke with who had unwittingly helped me.

Facts: HIV/AIDS

- Women and girls are more vulnerable to HIV/AIDS because of political, social and cultural inequality. At most risk are those trafficked into commercial sex. Sex trafficking is an almost inevitable death sentence for the victims:
  - Victims cannot insist on condom use and are vulnerable to dangerous sexual practices most associated with transmission.
  - They are forced to endure intercourse with multiple partners.
  - Violence is common in commercial sex and particularly prevalent when women or children are forcibly subjected to sex against their will. Injuries and abrasions sustained during sexual contact heighten physical vulnerability to HIV/AIDS transmission.
- The physically immature bodies of young girls are highly vulnerable to injuries, significantly heightening their risk of infection. Moreover, having other sexually transmitted diseases heightens the risk of contracting HIV/AIDS by up to a factor of ten.
- Coercing or forcing millions of women and children into violent, unprotected sex acts with multiple partners is a significant factor in the spread of the AIDS pandemic. The vulnerability of trafficked women to sexually transmitted diseases is compounded by their failure to receive medical testing, treatment, counseling, prevention services or other health care. The inability to speak or understand the language in a foreign land, poverty and indebtedness, and a lack of freedom all impede access to health care.
- While it is understood that prostitution and trafficking are significant contributors to the growth of AIDS, it is less understood that AIDS is a factor in the crime of sex trafficking, particularly the traffic in young girls. Men seek ever-younger partners or virgins to avoid becoming infected themselves, or in the mistaken belief that having sex with a virgin will cure a person with AIDS. With so many family breadwinners dead or ill, orphaned children and widows engage in survival sex, which places them at risk of the disease.
- Pressuring governments to end sex trafficking is an integral part of AIDS prevention.

16

Changes

A perfect cop never lets his job affect his emotions.
He can spend hours dealing with drunks, domestics, drug users, injured or dead
people, and then come home and be a loving,
well-adjusted husband and father. . . . I have never met a perfect cop.

Author unknown

I now routinely returned from overseas exhausted and completely drained. I was finding it increasingly difficult to be fully present emotionally and available to my wife. After working undercover on and off for nearly three years, some good friends from New Zealand visited us in the United States and were shocked at how much I had changed. I initially thought they were joking, but as time went on, it became apparent that they were very concerned about me. It was with some sadness that I realized that I had indeed forgotten how to play.

Things came to a head, of all places, in Disneyland. I had just returned from Southeast Asia, where I had documented the cases of several children who had been abducted and sold into prostitution. After only one day of international air travel, I was back in the United States and suddenly responsible for my friends' children. Tasked with negotiating crowds of strangers in what seemed like a very superficial and surreal environment, I naturally resorted to the skills I had acquired in the field. When I momentarily lost sight of the children as they were enveloped by a passing parade of Disney characters, I was only seconds away from jumping on Donald Duck and attacking Mickey Mouse.

PERSONAL TOLL

The personal toll on me and on my wife was growing insidiously. I originally viewed our marriage as being characterized as a knight in shining armor and his damsel in distress. I saw myself as someone who would rescue her and be her warrior, protector and hero.

Despite my marriage vows to the contrary, with every deployment I was increasingly becoming emotionally unavailable to Alice. Every day in the field meant another day where I was, by necessity, completely in control of my emotions and my actions. I was now finding it impossible to leave behind the emotionally guarded man I had become. By keeping to myself the trauma and the ugly atrocities that I witnessed, I believed I was protecting her. And after all, how would I even begin to speak about the unspeakable? Having been away for more than a month at a time, I wanted to be able to fully contribute and give myself to Alice on my return. What I found instead was that I needed even more time to be by myself.

I could not fathom the immense responsibility I was feeling for the victims yet to be rescued. With every deployment I met still more women and children who were desperate for some kind of outside intervention. The faces of those victims of trafficking I documented but had been unable to rescue continued to haunt me. Their desperate cries for rescue becoming an increasingly heavy burden to carry.

Being relatively successful at what I did also provided tremendous reinforcement to continue to pursue the goals and objectives of the organization. The responsibility I felt for those I had not been able to rescue colluded with an underlying belief that I could do more. The unfortunate result was that I unwittingly and unintentionally came to believe that the victims of trafficking needed me. In my own mind I had become their only hope.

This festering lie was to have dire consequences.

SECONDARY TRAUMA

I was also becoming increasingly frustrated with my immediate supervisor. I had been conducting missions in the developing world now for nearly four years, and I believed I knew what worked and what did not. I was facing very real risks to my own safety, and I felt unheard in relation to these concerns. His management style left me feeling that there was little room for discussion, and though I liked him very much, he was rapidly losing my respect.

In addition to this, though I did not know it at the time, during my last year while deployed overseas I was suffering from secondary trauma. I had unwittingly inhaled a dangerous cocktail of unrelenting stress, limited control over the outcomes of my work and a genuine sense of my own inadequacy in the face of the huge number of victims in desperate need of rescue. Vicarious, or "secondary," trauma is defined as "transformation of a person's inner experience as the result of empathetic engagement with another's trauma."

In other words, by spending time with, listening to and caring for victims suffering from psychological trauma, the caregiver or rescuer sometimes vicariously relives the original traumatic events themselves and suffers accordingly. Typically this displays itself through emotional shutdown or numbness, feeling disconnected from others, decreased ability to experience pleasure, hypervigilance and a failure to take care of oneself.

My motivation for doing this work had always been based on my belief that whatever I did for the most vulnerable and oppressed I was doing for God. I believed that by rescuing a child from a brothel I was accurately representing the true heart of God and his passion for justice. By default I also unconsciously believed and came to expect that, because I was doing God's work, he would protect my wife and me, and keep us safe from the fall-out of my work.

I was familiar with the writing of World War II holocaust survivor Corrie ten Boom who had written, "The center of His will is our only safety." Like many Christians, I had falsely translated this to mean that so long as we were doing God's will, we would all be safe. I did not know or understand at the time that these words were spoken from inside the horror of a Nazi concentration camp. I did not know that what she meant by these words was that no matter how evil our opposition, how horrific our suffering and how violent our death, that ultimately we remain untouchable in the hands of him who holds the keys to life.

Tragically, the danger was closing in around me, and it was to have a devastating effect. But the danger was not at all in the form that I had anticipated.

17

Caribbean

His Name Is Juan

Imagine a tropical island paradise in the Caribbean, complete
with warm, white sand, crystal clear, blue water and lush green
palm trees gently responding to the touch of a cool ocean breeze.
This is a developing country heavily dependent on tourism. The
small nation proudly promotes its one thousand miles of coastline
with white sand beaches, boating and diving attractions, and un-
spoiled nature.

Luxury all-inclusive resorts abound on the north, south and
east coasts. As the sun slowly sets on the Island of Capriola, the
tanned tourists and tired surfers withdraw to their resorts and
condominiums. As dusk settles the beach is quiet and vacant.

Vacant, that is, except for the bare feet of small children as
they slowly emerge from the growing shadows that stretch
across the sand. The tropical island paradise is about to become a market from hell, where the products being purchased
are children.

I was deployed here to investigate the extent of child sexual
exploitation and sex trafficking. I visited the southern resort
towns of Sangua and Priola as well as the northern beach towns.
In each tourist town and coastal village, I found the same thing: a

black market trade in the flesh of the vulnerable young girls and boys of the Caribbean.

In Sangua, in addition to the readily available young women and girls who prostituted themselves in the massage parlors, hotels and streets, I was also offered young boys. The youngest of these was Juan. In speaking to him alone it became apparent that he was only eight years old and was an orphan. He said he made his living by picking though the garbage for food scraps by day and being sodomized by sex tourists by night. Juan found community and support in the form of a local street gang. The gang sent him out each evening to be abused by visiting tourists in exchange for as little as $20. I gave Juan some money for food before he disappeared into the night. I added his name to the list of victims I hoped would be rescued in the coming weeks.

Other boys who frequented the beaches during the evenings came from a wide variety of dysfunctional homes and family backgrounds. Under the cover of darkness and with the sand still warm under their feet, the boys vied for the attention of tourists from North America, Europe and Asia.

In Priola I negotiated with a seemingly endless supply of pimps: men and women from all walks of life offering their nieces, their friends, their neighbors and their daughters in exchange for a quick profit. I also met and developed a rapport with a number of sex tourists from the United States. These were men who worked and saved hard all year in order to allow them to travel to the Caribbean for a few months of pleasure. There they gorged themselves on any and every fantasy, completely self-absorbed in their own world of hedonism and depravity. Many openly exchanged their stories of conquest, of carousing, abusing and, in some cases, raping their prey.

Lax and corrupt law enforcement meant that most of these predators were able to operate with impunity. The few who did get apprehended were invariably able to leave the country unpunished. These men looked like the proverbial boy next door. They were well spoken, in some cases well educated, and were of all shapes, races and ages. The only characteristic they all shared in common was an incessant and compulsive interest in their own pleasure.

An international undercover operation targeting the sex industry of this nation had never been done before. Before any intervention could be contemplated, a good working relationship with trusted police officers was essential. In addition, safe, reliable and professional aftercare providers and facilities had to be found to properly care for any victims rescued.

TARGET SANGUA

The organization I was working for limited the scope of the operation to one target: Sangua. As the scene of criminal activity closest to the capital city, it was believed this would facilitate greater cooperation on behalf of the local authorities. It was well known that the local law enforcement in Sangua was corrupt and that some officers were actively profiting from the sex trade. Officers from a different and unrelated unit would therefore be required for the operation.

I had returned to Sangua to reestablish old relationships with the pimps and child prostitutes I had met during my previous visit. The challenge lay in building sufficient rapport with those who were most heavily involved in the sale of the victims to be targeted by our operation. While making contact with the children being sold was relatively easy, it was more difficult to readily identify those who were selling them and making a profit from their ongoing abuse and exploitation.

To complete this task my help came in the form of José, a ten-year-old boy who was orphaned at a young age and who found himself being sold on the sandy beaches by older boys and men, before he escaped and fled to the city. There he was rescued by a missionary couple who cared for many of the children from the streets. While visiting the couple with a mutual friend who was acting as my translator, they communicated some of the horror that had befallen many of the children in their care, including José.

Given his knowledge of the abuse that took place in Sangua, I saw in José an amazing opportunity to utilize the knowledge and experience he had to further our mission. In talking with him through a translator it became apparent that José was terrified of returning to the beach he associated with so much evil and fear. His large brown eyes became animated and tearful as he described some of the teenage boys and men who still lived in Sangua.

I carefully described to José our desire to apprehend those men for their ongoing abuse of the boys and girls still living in Sangua. I explained how we would disguise and shield him in the back seat of a vehicle with tinted windows before driving through the area, only stopping long enough for him to point out the relevant people and places. Through my translator, I assured him of our protection. Ultimately we left him to consider my request, knowing that it would demand an immense amount of courage to even see some of the people and places where his nightmares were first born.

The following day I learned from his caregivers that José had agreed to be our guide. A small boy confronted the Goliath of the local commercial sex trade. José sat quietly beside his foster father in the back seat of our vehicle as we drove slowly through the streets and parks of Sangua. Though he sometimes reflexively ducked down to avoid the roving eyes of his former captors, José calmly pointed out key players in the sex industry.

He identified crucial locations where the exploitation occurred, and described in detail the relationships that existed between them. His knowledge of the underbelly of the small tourist town was invaluable to our proposed mission, and we could not thank him enough as we praised him for his bravery. Little José returned to his foster home that evening with a new strength, having looked his demons in the eye.

THE SEX PARTY

I subsequently returned to the hotels, parks, streets and beaches that José had identified and met many of the perpetrators he had singled out. I subsequently arranged for three groups of offenders to deliver some young girls and boys to a "turista cabana," or sex motel. Such motels are common throughout Latin America and are specifically designed to facilitate anonymous and discreet sexual liaisons. The Cabanas Tarde (Evening Cabins) was no different.

The motel was set out in two rows of units facing each other and separated only by the main driveway. Each unit had an adjacent garage that allowed customers to drive into the garage and close the door behind them. Once inside the motel units, payment was made through a slot in the wall, and towels and condoms were delivered the same way by the service staff. If I had learned nothing else during my time conducting these kinds of operations, it was this: use the perpetrators' system against them.

The first group of pimps initially consisted of three local young men who had individually and together supplied me with the offer of "young girls." Due to greed and their own infighting, one of the members was discarded by the other two early on. The second offender was a beach hustler who offered the sunbathing tourists anything from cocaine to children. The third perpetrator was a Haitian immigrant who acted as a chaperone and pimp for the boys living and working in the shadows of the beaches. With some cunning and careful planning, I was able to get the three groups to agree to arrive at the motel at prearranged times along with their victims.

At 8 a.m. the following morning, a Latino colleague and I met with and briefed a team of plainclothes police officers from the fraud division of the National Police. The commander spoke basic English and appeared to be an honest and conscientious man.

We had earlier hired three vans, each with tinted windows that were a common sight. These would be used to ferry the police teams into three of the six motel units I had rented for the day. Each garage was immediately adjacent to the other three motel units where the perpetrators would be directed. The tinted windows would allow for the officers to drive into the complex without raising the suspicions of the owners or motel staff. Once the offenders had arrived with their victims ready for sale, it was agreed that I would give the prearranged signal on the radio and the police would then raid each of the targets. Almost as an afterthought, I also said that if, for some reason, the radios did not work, I would use the car horn to signal the raid.

During the briefing the majority of the police officers seemed very receptive and motivated to do something about the problem. However we did not know what links any of them may have had with their colleagues in Sangua. We therefore asked all of the officers involved in the operation, with the exception of the commanding officer, to turn off their cell phones until after the raid was complete. We knew this would not guarantee that a tipoff would not occur. In addition to the police officers, a local federal prosecutor, a child advocate and government social workers were also in attendance. In a situation like this, none of their allegiances could be assured, and there were a lot of unknowns.

While traveling in convoy from the capital to Sangua, I received a call from the second offender, the beach hustler, to say that he had been beaten up by some of the parents of the children he had been endeavoring to sell. Apparently they had found out what he was planning to do with their children. It transpired that in addition to the children of the streets, he had solicited additional children from his neighborhood.

While I was frustrated at his incompetence, I was pleased the other children had not become involved. His decision to try to procure more children was not part of our original agreement, and had he been successful in doing so he may have been able to successfully defend himself at any subsequent criminal hearing on the basis of entrapment. I asked him to stick to the plan and said I would give him a ride myself from the main street in Sangua.

Each of the three vans carrying the raiding teams entered the hotel garages without incident and without raising any suspicion on behalf of the motel staff. At the prearranged time, the first of the pimps arrived. The first two offenders delivered fourteen girls between the ages of twelve and sixteen years. The Haitian pimp arrived with eight boys, the oldest of which was only twelve. I was thrilled to see that the youngest of the boys was eight-year-old Juan.

As they arrived, I confirmed with each of the offenders that they were delivering the children on the basis of the agreements previously made. I paid them the remainder of the deposit I had promised them for their efforts, and this was recorded on covert camera. I then urged them all to be as quiet as possible and once they were all safely ensconced in their respective units, I drove at speed into Sangua to pick up the beach hustler.

It was a nerve-racking journey. I was aware that any number of factors could foil the impending intervention. If the boys and girls within the units made too much noise, it was possible that one of the motel staff might ask them to leave. If any of the pimps strayed outside and identified the police officers secreted in the adjacent units, the intervention would be thwarted. I silently prayed, asking God to blind the eyes of the suspects to what we were planning.

INTERVENTION

With thoughts of all the things that could go wrong flying through my mind, I pulled up alongside the beach hustler and tried to appear calm as he ushered his two teenage girls, fourteen and sixteen years old, inside my vehicle. With my mind racing with the potential for disaster on many fronts, I headed back to the Cabanas as fast as I could, all the while engaging in what I hoped would appear to be a flirtatious exchange with the two girls seated behind me. With squealing tires I pulled up outside the gate of the motel again and a bemused security guard allowed me entry. There was no one in sight, which was a good indication that everything was going according to plan. The beach hustler along with his two victims disembarked from my vehicle and entered the remaining unit where I paid him the remainder of the deposit I owed him. I then closed the door and went to get my imaginary "clients."

When I went to give the signal, I found that the two-way radio supplied by the police did not work, and I was thankful for the backup plan. With adrenaline pumping and my nerves popping I jumped into my vehicle and leaned on the horn. I then watched as police officers ran from their hiding places with their guns drawn and stormed all three rooms. All four suspects were successfully apprehended and twenty-four victims of child sexual exploitation were rescued.

When the owner of the Cabanas saw what was happening, he barricaded himself in his office and called the local police to report a robbery. About five minutes later as I walked between the motel units, several armed men appeared at the gate of the motel. The police raiding team from the capital saw them and produced their own automatic weapons. The groups began screaming at each other to put their weapons down while, at the same time, acquiring potential targets. Fearing an imminent gun battle, I took cover behind a palm tree and watched with horror as the two groups came within seconds of opening fire on each other.

Thankfully, one of the police officers with us was in uniform, and when it was established that all were police officers, they put their guns away. With considerable relief, a tragedy was narrowly avoided.

For the first time in the history of this nation, four men were charged under the newly established sex-trafficking legislation. I subsequently received a death threat from one of the offenders. A small team of personal protection officers was assigned to me to ensure that I was able to safely testify against each of the four men. All four were convicted and sentenced to several years imprisonment. It was a major victory for the human rights community and for the local government.

While we savored the success of the prosecution, the aftercare of the victims was an abysmal failure. Within days of the operation, every one of the twenty-four children had run away, been released or asked to leave the respective aftercare facilities due to their "unruly" behavior. Despite our best efforts at screening the aftercare organizations concerned, it transpired that none of them was properly equipped or prepared to provide the specialized care that is required by victims of child sexual exploitation.

Juan, along with all of the other victims, returned to their lives in the shadows of the golden beaches of the Caribbean.

FACTS: *Aftercare*

- Victims of sex trafficking and forced prostitution have typically been isolated from their families, friends and home communities, and have suffered physical and sexual abuse, medical problems and the extreme trauma associated with living in slavery. The healing journey is usually intense and requires professional aftercare.

- The needs of children rescued from sexual slavery are especially challenging. In addition to trauma care, quality aftercare must address the safety and security of the children, facilitate a sense of belonging, healing and community for the children, and where possible, reintegrate them back into their family and society.

- In the developing world, there is a substantial lack of quality aftercare programs and places of safety where rescued victims can be placed. Many government aftercare shelters are completely inadequate, and some victims choose to run away as a result. This frustrates the prosecution process because, without the testimony of the victims, criminal charges against the perpetrators cannot be proven.

- In some cases, victims have been abducted from the aftercare centers by the very same perpetrators who originally enslaved them. Without a safe and secure aftercare center, any intervention resulting in the rescue of victims from commercial sexual exploitation is likely to fail.

- Hagar International is a global aftercare provider that has worked with some of the children rescued by the author. Their model offers a long-term holistic approach resulting in successful prosecutions and resilient children through personal transformation, social reintegration and economic empowerment.

This chart was provided to the author and is used courtesy of Hagar International <www.Hagarinternational.org>.

18

The Cost

We set out to save the Shire,
and it has been saved, . . . but not for me.

The Fellowship of the Ring

When I was deployed to Kedang Tebal, the information provided
by the two Thai investigators had suggested that the only way to safely
speak to some of the trafficking victims was to take them offsite to
a hotel, away from the criminals who carefully monitored them.

This presented all kinds of potential challenges. The covert cameras we carried were not only used to gather evidence; they also afforded us a means of protection from any subsequent spurious allega-
tions of sexual misconduct on the part of the victim or the trafficker.
After all, what better way to discredit the evidence of a potential witness like me than by alleging that I furthered the criminal exploitation of the victim by using her sexually. Taking a girl back to my room
for the night necessarily meant that I would be in close proximity to
her for a longer period of time than the covert cameras could record.

Given my experience in the field, I was confident of my own
ability to control myself and saw it merely as another challenge or
occupational hazard to be overcome. The first call I made was to
the director of our Southeast Asia office. I discussed the proposed
operation with him as well as the potential risks. He gave me the

green light, and recognizing the huge potential to compromise myself, he offered to pray for me.

The second call I made was to my wife. I knew Alice could well see things very differently. I explained to her that the only way I could get the necessary information to rescue the victims in this particular case was to have one of the girls spend the night with me in my hotel room. Alice simply said, "What choice do I have?" What I did not know and would only find out years later was that my call left her feeling devastated and that she later broke down and wept bitterly.

I had given her no prior warning and had contacted her in the knowledge that her response could potentially facilitate or thwart the rescue of many. Alice spent a sleepless night in New York, aware that not only was her husband engaging in a very dangerous investigation but that he was also spending the entire night alone in his hotel room with a prostitute.

I failed to realize at the time that no matter what the outcome of the operation and whether I proved myself faithful to Alice or not, our relationship and our marriage would never be the same again. My willingness to take this step for the sake of the investigation was crossing a line that put my work before her and before our marriage.

Due to the time difference, I had to wait several hours the following day before I could call Alice and update her. She sounded both tired and relieved to hear my voice. As I hung up the telephone, I was only faintly aware of an unspoken barrier that had arisen between us.

SUCCESSFUL

It was very easy for me to believe that God was on my side, especially given the largely successful operations in Southeast Asia and in other parts of the world resulting in the liberation of many hundreds of victims and the prosecution and incarceration of many perpetrators.

I left the region, as I did following every deployment, believing that with every operation I was getting morally stronger. After all, I had just demonstrated that I could sleep in the same bed with a beautiful prostitute and not have sex with her. I reasoned that my ability to withstand the seduction and the temptation was in part what made me an effective investigator. I was still sensitive enough to feel truly heartbroken for the plight of the victims of trafficking I was meeting, and my passion to fight for them was only growing stronger.

What I did not realize was that my moral compass was spinning. With every operation, I was in fact becoming more and more ensnared by the sex industry and all its associated trappings. It is for this very reason that many organizations working in the area of sex trafficking have developed clear and defined boundaries around appropriate touch for their undercover investigators. With every naked body I saw, every flirtatious kiss I returned and every sensual touch I felt, I was becoming increasingly desensitized to the darkness. What I thought was making me stronger was in fact eroding the very foundation on which I stood.

Twice when deployed in Southeast Asia, I had kissed girls when I thought it necessary to maintain my cover and to further the ruse being played out between us. This convinced the girls, as well as the criminals looking on, that I was authentic and that my interest was purely sexual, like so many of those around me. The last thing I wanted to do was stand out by going into a brothel or go-go bar and then behaving like a prude. My safety relied on coming across as the person I was pretending to be.

What I was not aware of was the fact that, with every kiss and every touch, I was moving further and further down the continuum of sexual intimacy. I was engaging in behavior that I had only ever contemplated with my wife. Without the assistance of an objective handler or anyone properly debriefing or otherwise monitoring me, I could easily justify what I was doing on the grounds of safety and successful rescues. Unfortunately, I was only fooling myself.

With every kiss, I felt more and more estranged from Alice. With every touch from another woman, my marriage vows seemed less binding. The unwavering faithfulness and devotion I had once promised her was being slowly eroded and condensed, until all that was left was a commitment not to have intercourse with anyone other than her. Everything else had become a "necessary evil" to further the work of abolition and rescue.

My own judgment was becoming increasingly clouded as to what physical contact was a necessary part of my "cover" and what was simply an extremely pleasurable perk of the job. Agreeing to kiss a woman at the encouragement of a major trafficker, while sitting inside his fortified and heavily guarded brothel, may seem like the wise thing to do. However, the male body's natural response to the kiss is still one of pleasure, and a heightened degree of intimacy is inevitable. What kissing and touching was therefore required to complete the mission, and what I just enjoyed, became impossible to differentiate.

With the benefit of hindsight, it seems only natural that this should occur. In the same way that undercover police officers infiltrating the drug scene often become addicted to the very drugs they set out to contain, so too was the sex industry beginning to work its way into my heart and mind. Immersed in a world of living pornography, the images and faces and bodies that were offered to me began to bombard my thinking and my dreaming.

While I maintained many healthy friendships with men at work and within my neighborhood and community, at another level I was feeling increasingly isolated and cut off from those around me. I was at a loss as to how to communicate all that I experienced. I felt I could not tell Alice about the challenges I was facing that had become a regular part of my deployments. I was uncomfortable with the changes taking place within me, yet at the same time I was impatient to return to those who I knew were desperate for rescue.

Ultimately, perhaps, the image I had of myself as "rescuing hero" won out over "faithful husband," and I continued to take even greater risks and lead even more dangerous missions.

19

Caribbean

Her Name Is Carla

*He who fights with monsters should see to it
that he himself does not become a monster.
For when you gaze long into an abyss,
the abyss also gazes into you.*

Friedrich Nietzsche

Everything changed for me in the Caribbean. Everything.

I arrived in the capital and commenced my investigation as I had on every other mission and international deployment. I first met with a variety of people who provided me with local intelligence and information on the culture, geography and criminal justice system.

This particular country has a long history of piracy, prostitution and slavery. While their nature and form have changed, these same vices are still very apparent today. Pirates still patrol the surrounding waters and attack people with automatic weapons, stealing money and valuables. Indeed the country has been dubbed the murder capital of the world. Most murders are gang-related. The country is dominated by a small number of Mafia-style criminal gangs, who allegedly control various parts of the capital city as well as some political parties and industries throughout the country. Corruption is rife, and the rule of law is at times very tenuous.

It did not take long for me to locate modern-day slavery. I had only just checked into my hotel when I was approached by a Rastafarian man who introduced himself as Jah Pete. Describing himself as a national folk hero, he said he was a reggae performer as well as a popular community worker. He showed me a folder full of certificates, plaques and newspaper clippings detailing the work he had performed in the community and the money he had made through his recordings on behalf of children in the community. One of his songs was titled "Every Child Needs a Mother and a Father." Jah Pete then conceded that he had fathered eight children with as many different women. However he saw nothing incongruous in this.

To supplement his reggae music career, Jah Pete admitted that he also received income from helping visitors to his country access whatever they desired. In addition to illegal narcotics, he offered me the sexual services of girls as young as thirteen.

True to his word, Jah Pete subsequently arrived at my hotel with two girls, age thirteen and fifteen. I took the three of them out to lunch and learned that both girls were poor, fatherless and desperate. One of them was an aspiring singer, and she treated me to an afternoon of love songs and hymns. I recorded Jah Pete on camera receiving a deposit for the sexual services of both girls.

On the streets surrounding my hotel, men of a similar ilk were in abundance. I could not walk within twenty feet of the front gate without being offered all manner of women, drugs and gold jewelry. Over the course of the coming days, I captured numerous transactions on camera as well as several interviews with some of the young girls.

STING OPERATION

I subsequently met with and arranged for members of the local police to set up a sting operation inside my hotel. I continued to communicate with several of the pimps who had offered me girls as young as thirteen to purchase for the night. For their part the police were very willing to participate. The government had yet to introduce trafficking legislation and was also coming under considerable international pressure to more effectively combat the prostitution of children.

I arranged for Joanne, a local woman whom I had previously met, to act on behalf of any victims rescued. Joanne was a professional woman and headed her own organization. Covert cameras were set up inside the hotel room to be utilized, and I briefed a team of six officers from the local constabulary. They then secreted themselves around the hotel, and we waited.

At the prearranged time, two male pimps showed up with a thirteen-year-old girl named Carla. After meeting them in the car park at the rear of the hotel, I walked them past the main restaurant and pool area where the plainclothes police officers were sitting, and into my hotel room.

After confirming the details of the arrangement again for the sake of the video evidence, I paid the two men their asking price of $300. Having paid the men and completed the transaction, I opened the door to an adjoining room and two police officers came in with their guns drawn and arrested the two suspects. I quickly ushered Carla into the next room where Joanne was waiting to provide reassurance and support.

The operation went very smoothly, and the marked money was located on the two suspects. One of the officers had also listened to the conversation from the adjoining room. The men's cell phones were seized along with their other personal possessions. The agreement was captured by two video cameras and copies of the video were forwarded to the police for their use in any subsequent prosecution.

The two offenders were transported to the police station while

I accompanied Joanne and Carla. Once she had been debriefed, it became apparent that Carla had in fact just turned fourteen but had been told to say she was thirteen by the offenders. She was recruited by one of the two men who lived near her home.

While the sting operation had been successful, my primary target was not the prostitution of children but human trafficking.

DEMONS SING

I began targeting those clubs known to be selling women from Eastern Europe. Inside a strip club named Ecstasy I met a woman from Ukraine. Her working name was Tanya and she said she was twenty-seven years old. She explained that it had cost her $2,000 for her air tickets and that, before she could leave the country, she had to pay this back to the owners of the club. However, she indicated that she had already paid off $1,000, as well as sending money home to her impoverished mother. Tanya said she would pay off the other $1,000 and then save some more money before returning home.

As the week progressed, I purchased the time of three further Ukrainian women from three different bars. I took each of them back to my hotel room where I covertly recorded their stories. They had similar tales to tell of grinding poverty and desperation. With nothing to lose, each had made the decision to return to make some money.

There were elements of coercion involved in that they each had to surrender their passports and were not allowed to leave the country until they had paid off their debts. However, each of the women also stated that they knew the nature and conditions of their work before they arrived and that they were treated well by the bar owners. Some talked openly about the dangers of sex trafficking but did not consider themselves to be victims of such.

During my last night in the capital, I visited the Camelot go-go bar. There I met another woman from Ukraine who said her name was Katya. While it was difficult to talk amid the deafening music and strobe lights, Katya seemed somewhat disengaged from the role she was playing, and I thought I sensed in her the faint signs of someone who was not happy to be there. She was blond, in her late twenties, very beautiful and carried herself with a quiet maturity that I was immediately drawn to.

After I inquired about her price Katya introduced me to the bar owner, a man named Junior. Junior was a soft-spoken and well-educated man who was clearly making a lot of money. He showed me a freshly decorated ground floor area that he said he was turning into a casino. Junior explained that once he had the carpet down, he planned to install a number of gambling machines in the coming month.

I paid Junior the $300 asking price for Katya. While she went to change into her street clothes, I explained to Junior that I was planning to bring a group of men for a vacation. Junior offered to supply whatever women I required and further said that, by the time they arrived, he would have additional girls from the Dominican Republic and Colombia. Knowing that both countries were common sources of trafficked women, I believed I was finally onto something.

As Katya returned and we prepared to leave, Junior handed me a flyer advertising a bikini car wash and wet T-shirt competition scheduled for the following weekend. With this in hand, I duly escorted Katya from the premises and drove her back to my hotel.

As I had done several hundred times before all around the world, I explained to the woman sitting opposite me that I had only recently separated and that I was not looking for sex but merely desired her company. Katya accepted this and began to tell me her story.

Katya indicated that the first time she came, she had been forced to pay off a debt before she could leave. However she had paid the debt and returned to Ukraine where she had been able to support her impoverished family with her savings. This was her second time into the country, and this time she was working for herself. She now operated as an independent contractor, only had a verbal agreement with the owners of the Camelot and that there was nothing in writing. Katya explained that she had just returned from a four-day vacation on the western side of the island, where she had stayed with her friends.

Katya said she only agreed to go with those men that she wanted to accompany and that she never went with any local men. She said that she was never forced to go with anyone she did not want to. She explained that she was on good terms with the owners and they treated her well.

From our conversation it was becoming apparent that while Katya had experienced a form of coercion in the past, she was not currently a victim of trafficking. Having worked in the industry already, she simply saw it as a means to be able to make some good money for her impoverished parents.

As Katya talked about her love for her family and how much she missed her homeland, I began to feel an affinity with her. I also felt compassion for this beautiful young woman, sacrificing so much of herself and her life in order to support her family. From our conversation it was becoming apparent that while Katya had experienced a form of coercion in the past, she was not in any legal sense currently a victim of trafficking.

I explained to Katya again that I did not want sex and asked if she would be happy to give me a back massage instead. While she was in the bathroom I subtly turned off the covert camera, disappointed that I had not been able to locate any firm trafficking leads in the capital. As I removed my shirt and lay down on the bed for my massage, Katya emerged from the bathroom wearing only a towel.

Unlike many of the women from whom I had endured a "massage" during my four years undercover, Katya was good.

Indeed she knew how to push me in places I did not know existed. The massage was very effective and I began to relax both my body and my guard. I had been away from home for six months on this deployment and the warm touch of a woman felt fantastic. Without warning, Katya lay down beside me and placed my hand on her breast. Within moments she was climbing on top of me. I protested verbally, but only verbally, and then not at all.

My faith embodied who I was and had changed the way I lived and how I saw the world. It had led me to my wife, and it had led me to this undercover work. I had spent my life pursuing an authentic and very genuine relationship with God, and I despised all forms of hypocrisy and pretense. I had publicly stated that light was stronger than darkness and had espoused the need for more men to join me by fearlessly infiltrating brothels and rescuing those held captive. I was a committed husband and believed in the sanctity of marriage, in faithfulness and fidelity. This was who I was.

Within the space of five seconds, I betrayed all that I was, all that I stood for and believed in as well as my marriage vows, my wife, my integrity, my role, my very life and, ultimately, my God.

Katya could see that I was in shock and asked what was wrong. I quickly and kindly dismissed her concern and got dressed. I transported her back to the Camelot before returning in an anguished daze to my hotel room. As I closed the door behind me, I sank to the floor and wept.

Amid the self-condemnation I heard a kind of demonic laughter in my ears that was almost audible: "We finally got you. You who believed light was stronger than darkness. Well, we finally got you."

The minutes turned into hours, and the hours turned into days. The shame that I had witnessed engulf the lives of so many others was now consuming me from the inside. I was gripped by gut-wrenching despair and overwhelmed with guilt and palpable pain.

I tried to function, but the smallest task seemed suddenly insur-
mountable. I felt like I had been hit by a truck.

I wrestled with how I was going to tell Alice what had happened and how she would respond.

I was utterly and completely broken.

Facts: Women

- Women have endured a unique hatred over the years: foot binding, genital mutilation, religious and social segregation, denial of education and voting rights, sexual violence, rape, prostitution. Indeed, being viewed as a commodity to be purchased is perhaps nothing new.

- A girl who has lost her virginity, even through rape, is considered to be "damaged goods." "A girl who is raped . . . will frequently be burdened with the shame of no longer being a virgin. For some . . . it is a shame that leaves them no option other than to become a prostitute because they honestly believe that they are no longer worthy enough to become the wife of a decent man."

- Rape is commonly used as an initiation into prostitution.

  A raped girl is unable to marry because she is no longer a virgin. Such women resort to sex work because it is the only form of work available to them and because they cannot survive as single women. Ironically, the trauma of the rape and the devastating consequences that flow from it can sometimes bind the girl to her rapist. The perpetrator of the crime then becomes her trafficker and her pimp. In other words he creates the prostitute and then he profits from her.

- In many cultures it is easier to rescue women from forced prostitution than to remove the shame from their soul. Branded in the eyes of their community, many women feel permanently dishonored and disgraced by their experiences. "Prostitution for women is a sin from which there is no absolution and no return. . . . This applies whether a woman chose to sell sex, . . . was forced by economic circumstances, or . . . was physically coerced."

- Women are locked into brothels by social shame: "The internalization of the bad woman image is one of the most effective chains tying women into sex work. . . . There can be few greater injustices than the stigmatization of prostitutes in societies in which many, and sometimes most men, buy sex."

20

Amazing Grace

But while he was still a long way off, his father saw him
and was filled with compassion for him; he ran to his son,
threw his arms around him and kissed him.

Luke 15:20

Shame is a powerful weapon and a brutal enemy. Its chains are thicker than any iron and it enslaves more harshly than a cruel dictator. Having thwarted criminals and outwitted slave masters, I now confronted my most formidable foe. The temptation to surrender to something so powerful was simply overwhelming, and for several days I could do little else but to submit to the condemnation and gut-wrenching despair.

During this time, I received a telephone call from a pastor in New Zealand. I confessed what had happened, and into my darkness he held out cleansing, forgiveness and absolution. It was then that I recalled the words I had first heard in my youth, the words that had first enticed me to follow this path of adventure and life abundant: "The love and grace of God is a free gift and there is nothing you can do to earn it; but it will cost you everything."

Strangely, it was no longer the excitement or the anticipation of the cost or even the challenge that held me, but the promise of grace; everything forgiven and an undeserved fresh start with no strings attached.

I initially resisted, the last strands of my identity defiantly clasping onto the image of a strong and powerful hero, reluctant to accept the weakness and frailty of my mortal humanity. My friend gently explained that the greater tragedy would be for me to presume that, unlike every other human being on earth, I was somehow disqualified from receiving the same gift of freedom, hope and forgiveness. Finally, I tearfully accepted the free gift offered to me. As I did so, the shame that had begun to make itself at home in my heart retreated.

I left the Caribbean and, after completing my contract in the United States, returned to New Zealand and to my extended family. After four years in the field of antitrafficking work, I resumed my role as a detective in the New Zealand Police. We had sold our home prior to leaving New Zealand, and during our time overseas the housing market had doubled in price. We were homeless, emotionally spent and financially broke, but ultimately thankful to be safely home and in the company of extended family and friends.

BEYOND REPAIR

I was determined to take whatever time we needed to put our marriage first for a season. For the next two years we tried to stop the tears, bind up the wounds and heal from the pain unintentionally inflicted during my time away from home. We went to marriage courses, marriage counselors and consumed marriage books. We talked and argued and fought and loved and forgave all over again and again and again. Sadly, the unseen barriers created during these four years remained between us, and it seemed as if the damage was irreversible.

I sensed that Alice felt as if there was no room for her in the marriage. I had already had an affair with my work and my role as an undercover investigator. I had been so willing to leave her for weeks at a time to complete my missions. She asked me to put aside my involvement with human slavery and trafficking while we focused on rebuilding our marriage.

However, I had changed as a result of the things I had seen and done. I was no longer the carefree, easygoing and fun-loving man she married. I remained passionate about the work of emancipation and rescue, and was quick to accept offers to speak publicly about the slavery I had witnessed. I hoped that by doing so others would join in the fight to see women and children set free and criminals brought to justice.

I also continued to keep in contact with many of my friends and contacts around the world involved in the work of antitrafficking. I found it difficult to let go of the role I once had and looked forward to exploring new opportunities for involvement and adventure. When I lacked the energy to play and seemed somehow to have lost the ability to relax, all of this ongoing activity was a bitter pill for Alice to swallow.

Our relationship deteriorated and the conflict between us only increased.

SEPARATION

Finally, Alice asked me again to tell her honestly the full extent of what I had done during my time in the bars and the brothels. Looking her in the eye, for the first time I tearfully told her the whole truth. I began with my first mission to the provocative go-go bars and seductive brothels of Southeast Asia, my moral confusion in Latin America, the numerous boundaries that were broken along the way, and, ultimately, my final betrayal in the Caribbean. I had put myself in harm's way and harm had caught up with me.

By the time I was through, a great weight had been lifted from me, and I was hopeful that this cleansing and honesty would be the key to unlock the door that had closed between us. I asked for her forgiveness and for the chance to start all over again.

But Alice was completely devastated and shocked. This was a betrayal of all I had promised her, and the deceit she had experienced at my hand was something she had never anticipated. With the erosion of trust between us, there was little room for negotiation or compromise. She filed for separation shortly thereafter, and out of respect for her wishes, I moved out of the family home. Our marriage was over.

The cost had suddenly become too great. We entered into the all-too-familiar suffering of those whose hearts are torn apart. I had spent four years of my life trying to defend and protect vulnerable women and alleviate their suffering. Yet here in the safety of our suburban New Zealand home, my own wife was now suffering as a result of my choices.

This was not how the story was supposed to end.

The next year was to be the worst year of our lives. Alice and I were committed to maintaining a healthy line of communication, and we did so. But the grief for both of us was at times all-consuming. Our understanding of God and his purposes on earth was shattered. The tearing apart of our marriage and our very souls was at times excruciating.

Alice has her own story, and it is not mine to tell. She was the one who trusted me, who endured sleepless nights praying for my safe return, who struggled to make ends meet with insufficient financial resources, and who was ultimately betrayed. Absolutely everything I say is written in the light of her silent tears and lonely suffering.

BATMAN WAS WRONG

During this season of loss, some significant things happened. By necessity, I was forced to let go of all those victims I had failed to rescue. I could no longer carry the combined weight of all the women and children I had vowed to go back for. And in doing so

I realized, of course, that they were never mine to carry in the first place.

Without the pressure of being constantly on guard and away from home, and with the help of my extended family, I slowly began to relax and learn once again how to play. The intensity and urgency in me slowly dissipated, and my easygoing nature began to return.

I was initially afraid of the tight grip of sorrow and grief, and thought they would forever pull me under. But I slowly learned to accept their embrace, and with the support of family and friends I was able to stay afloat. Strangely, I now found solace and strength in the company of friends whose lives had been similarly shattered by the suffering and unfairness of life. A young married couple who had lost their child to cancer. A son whose father had committed suicide. A man whose wife had been unfaithful. Those for whom life had not turned out quite as they had planned or dreamed.

Author John Eldredge talks of this unlikely source of strength:

> True strength does not come out of bravado. Until we are broken, our life will be self-centered, self-reliant; our strength will be our own. . . . I don't trust a man who hasn't suffered; I don't let a man get close to me who hasn't faced his wound. Think of the posers you know—are they the kind of man you would call at 2 a.m. when life is collapsing around you? Not me. I don't want clichés; I want deep, soulful truth, and that only comes when a man has walked the road I've been talking about.

I slowly surrendered the superhero I had been pursuing all my life. In doing so I found the freedom to be me, all of me, including my frailty, faults and failures. By accepting my simple humanity, my wound and my brokenness, I was also able to accept my need of others.

Ultimately I learned that Batman was wrong. It is not what we do that defines us. It is what God does in and through us. He does not simply want to be our personal Savior, but the Savior of the whole world. He not only desires to set us free from sin and all else that sucks abundant life from us, but to also liberate those held in physical bondage and tangible slavery. We are his hands and his feet on this earth. We are his rescue plan.

My idea of what it meant to be heroic also changed. John Eldredge writes: "[Our] culture comes along with figures like John Wayne and James Bond and all those other 'real men,' and the one thing they all have in common is that they are loners, they don't need anyone. We have come to believe deep in our hearts that needing anyone for anything is a sort of weakness, a handicap." I discovered that accepting my broken humanity and humbly asking for help is the most heroic step a man can take.

Finally, I was also invited, challenged even, to forgive myself. To treat myself with the same compassion I had afforded others. I staked my life on the fact and had boldly proclaimed that those imprisoned inside a brothel were not defined by their enslavement or their shame, but by their inherent dignity as human beings, as deeply loved children of God. I was now given the same opportunity to step out of the poison and the lies of that which condemned me. I was now able to protect my own heart whenever I was tempted to feel contaminated or otherwise disqualified from ever being loved and pursuing my dreams again.

I am so thankful that this is not the end of the story. I do not and cannot justify my actions. I alone am responsible for what happened and for the choices I made. I deeply regret some of the things that occurred during my time working undercover. With the benefit of hindsight, I would change many things if I were given the opportunity to do it all again. I carry with me every day the betrayal of my wife, the violation of my marriage vows and the pain I have caused Alice.

But grace is the free gift of undeserved forgiveness, cleansing, acceptance and wild, extravagant love. It is the promise of hope for every man, woman and child imprisoned by their frail and fallible humanity. This gift had allowed so many to walk with their heads held high from the degradation and humiliation of a brothel. I chose to follow their courageous example, and I refuse to listen to the voices of accusation and condemnation that would have me hide in my own dark prison for the rest of my days. Like them, I refuse to be enslaved or defined by shame.

When I was a boy listening to an invitation to adventure, I had no idea it would be so painful. I had no idea it would cost me and those I love so dearly. I had no understanding of how powerful and how devastating the dark hand of evil can be. But I also failed to understand why it was that this grace was so amazing and how it could be that this unlikely gift would ultimately triumph over my fear and shame.

My favorite movie scene is from *The Passion of the Christ*. The bloodied form of Jesus is staggering under the weight of the cross during the grueling forced march from Jerusalem to Golgotha. At one point he stumbles and falls to the ground, and his mother, Mary, has the opportunity to kneel beside him on the dusty road while the hostile crowd looks on. Jesus then utters the seemingly incongruous words when his swollen, disfigured face looks up, and he says, "See, Mother, I make all things new." It is an ironic yet powerful picture of God's grace and power, present in and triumphing over the greatest darkness in history and humanity's greatest shame.

THE GREATEST DANGER

I thought that the greatest challenges I had faced were inside the brothels of the developing world. I assumed that it was while working undercover that I was in the greatest danger. But I was wrong. The greatest challenge I faced was when I had "fallen from grace" and was tempted to allow shame and condemnation to become a part of who I was. The greatest danger I faced was when I was emotionally bankrupt and spiritually broken, and considered myself unworthy and unforgivable.

I am no superhero. I have many more questions now than when I first began. But I do now know, from what I have witnessed and indeed from what I have lived, that all things can be made new. And I know that it is actually in my redeemed and rescued humanity that I am dangerous and a force to be reckoned with. So I have hope. Hope for all those who are still imprisoned and oppressed. And I am still in this fight and still running in this race, knowing I still have something to contribute while there is life left in me.

For many people, and for many religions the world over, the idea that God is vulnerable and that God suffers is both offensive and repugnant. However, having seen what I have seen and done what I have done, I can only love and respect a God who has also known great suffering, betrayal, abandonment and loss.

I met this God in the terrified eyes of Lan and Milan in Southeast Asia. I met him again in the dead eyes of women in the Caribbean. I saw him in the tears of a small girl waving me goodbye from the doorstep of a tiny brothel in Latin America. And when I had betrayed everything I believed in, everyone who trusted me and everyone I held dear, I felt the embrace, cleansing and freedom of this God who makes all things new.

Some of those closest to me have expressed their concerns about me writing such an honest account of my experiences overseas. They fear that I will be judged by those quick to condemn. They are also worried about how my experiences and example will be interpreted by those who look up to me, my nieces and nephews and other children and young people whom I care about very much.

I have carefully considered their argument because, of course, I am also concerned that I may cause them unnecessary embarrassment. I care very deeply about their character, their moral development and maturity. I want to do everything I can to help them avoid making choices that will cause them, and those they love, unnecessary pain.

But I want so much more for them than a cautious, safe and untainted personal development. I want them to live fully aware of the fact that God knows they will make mistakes and anticipates that they will sometimes suffer. But like young Betsie ten Boom, who during World War II found herself inside the horror of a Nazi concentration camp, I want them to know with all their being that there is "no pit so deep that [God] is not deeper still."

When they do fall or choose unwisely, when life with all its unfairness ambushes them, and when they find themselves walking through dark valleys, I want those children to know that they are still pursued and adored by their Maker. I long for them to know in the core of their being that there is nothing they can do that will separate them from that love. I want them to know that all things can be made new: *"My grace is sufficient for you, for my power is made perfect in weakness"* (2 Corinthians 12:9). And in that knowledge I want them to live full, courageous, free and abundant lives.

FACTS: *Globalization*

- Globalization is the process by which businesses and investment capital move beyond domestic borders to markets around the globe, increasing the interconnectedness of different markets and populations. The commercial sexual exploitation of women and children has flourished across the globe thanks to the ease of conducting business around the world.

- In his book *Not for Sale*, David Batstone explains that sophisticated communication tools and relaxed banking laws have made it easy to exchange assets (including women and children) internationally. He writes, "Virtual enterprises can operate everywhere and nowhere, making themselves known only when and where they choose. . . . The capital flows to wherever it can most easily exploit cheap labour."

- Women and children of the Third World are especially vulnerable to the effects of this global economy. Poverty in the supply countries forces people to explore every possible way to improve their economic situation. Many victims of trafficking begin with the expectation that they will find legitimate employment, only to find enslavement instead. Similarly, those with resources in the developed world who are seeking to prey sexually on the vulnerability of others can do so with relative simplicity.

- A study on human trafficking done at Johns Hopkins revealed:

  > Traffickers, taking advantage of transparent borders, broadband communication, and political and economic upheaval as well as mass migrations of people, have preyed on the vulnerable [and] . . . have made trafficking into a booming business as well as a tragic fixture of our times. . . . The continued treatment of millions of women and children as a commodity . . . speaks volumes of the global community's failure to offer protection and opportunity across gender and age. The rapid proliferation of human trafficking and related brutality casts a dark shadow over the benefits that globalization has offered to many. Globalization has made the world a smaller place, but at a cost to many of the most vulnerable.

21

Mission Possible

To dream the impossible dream,
To fight the unbeatable foe, . . .
To be willing to march into Hell, for a Heavenly cause.

The Man from La Mancha

Despite all of the challenges and associated difficulties with sex trafficking, compared to other crimes it is relatively easy to effectively combat. Indeed, rescuing women and children and prosecuting the perpetrators responsible is very achievable. This is because there are several things about the sex industry that make it unique.

For those who profit from the sexual exploitation of women and children, the customer is both their largest asset and their greatest liability. Without the customer to purchase sex, there would be no sale and no profit. In order to make any money from selling their "products," the traffickers must first open their doors and allow customers to enter their domain. This necessarily exposes them, their staff and their business operation to anyone interested in documenting their activities and using that information to facilitate an intervention. There is just no other way around it.

UTILIZING THEIR WEAKNESSES
I found that there are very few places that cannot be infiltrated. The

criminals involved in this form of human slavery are primarily interested in the profits. As long as the purchase price is paid, they are generally content. Some establishments are more difficult in that they only cater to a very select clientele, such as very wealthy men or to men of a particular race. For example, I found one such bar in Southeast Asia that only allowed Japanese men to enter, initially thwarting our efforts. However, with the assistance of a Japanese police officer, this challenge was also overcome.

The male clients who use the sexual services of enslaved women and children are well aware that what they are doing is illegal. They therefore insist on a degree of anonymity and rely on being able to enter and leave such premises with the least amount of scrutiny. From the perspective of the investigator, this is a huge weakness and one that can be used to his advantage.

I was able to move with relative impunity through layers of security and detection simply by using the operating procedures of the brothels against them. In almost every brothel in the world there are opportunities for investigators to similarly enter such places of deprivation and abuse. The necessary evidence can be then gathered right under the noses of those criminals involved, simply by talking to the victims and then acting on their behalf.

From my own observations and work in the field, I think that what is most astounding is not that we were able to infiltrate brothels and rescue women and children, but rather that around the world so few people are doing so.

Those criminals making profits from trafficking have a further flaw in their business plans. Unlike drugs and weapons that cannot speak, the women and children who are the victims of this crime are always going to be potential prosecution witnesses. With the right kind of intervention, support and aftercare, their intimate knowledge of the criminals and their crimes makes every rescued victim a credible and reliable witness. They are every criminal's worst nightmare.

If properly cared for, protected and fully debriefed, each victim of trafficking can provide conscientious investigators with the details they require: how and where the victims were recruited and by whom, how they were transported, the descriptions of those corrupt officials who were involved, and the modus operandi of the criminal enterprise ultimately responsible for their enslavement.

Sadly, in many countries the police, customs and immigration officers are sometimes too eager to punish those women found working in the sex industry. They often remain unidentified as victims of trafficking simply because no one asks the right questions or digs beneath the surface. Without the appropriate level of reassurance and some guarantee of safety, most women who find themselves in this situation will not voluntarily disclose the full nature of their captivity. The key witnesses to the crimes are therefore often deported. In the event that a prosecution is mounted against the traffickers, they are subsequently discharged without conviction due to a lack of evidence.

OPERATIONAL EFFECTIVENESS

The infiltration and investigation of human trafficking is, by its very nature, extremely dangerous physically, morally and emotionally. Those involved must have the necessary qualifications, training and experience. In the face of such evil, there is always the temptation to take the law into your own hands. However, I cannot stress enough the absolute necessity of working in cooperation with local law enforcement. Anything other than this may be successful in the short term but will ultimately have long-term negative consequences and undermine those working to end human trafficking.

Like any enforcement action, it is vital to properly care for and protect the rescuers. This includes those on the front lines as well as the support staff in any organization. For example, it was one thing for me to record my interactions with criminals selling me small children for sex. It was another matter altogether for a typist or photographer who had no investigative training or experience to then spend hours reliving the crimes as they worked with the documentary and video evidence. All those involved in the traumatic and hazardous work of rescue require mandatory care and professional support.

The criminal networks involved in the commercial sexual exploitation of women and children range from multibillion dollar enterprises to very small businesses. Whatever the size or method of operation, because those involved are committing extreme forms of criminal human rights abuse, they are usually willing to take whatever action is necessary to protect their financial interests as well as avoid detection and prosecution. Their actions therefore are calculated, inhumane and utterly ruthless. And they are very committed to what they do.

Any investigative effort must be aware of this and must proactively conduct their operations accordingly. In some countries where I worked, the motto of those responsible for investigating such crimes seemed to be "hope for the best." Whatever the perceived size or scope of the criminal target under investigation, the complete picture will seldom be fully understood. This is especially so when interacting and operating within foreign cultures. Given the risks involved, the universal maxim of any effective intervention must always be "plan for the worst." Anything less is unprofessional and unlikely to succeed.

This specifically applies to the moral integrity of those staff involved in such investigations. The undercover operators are deployed into a world that is sexually charged, extremely seductive, devoid of constraints and overwhelmingly enticing. Speaking from experience, the very best of intentions held by those with the very highest moral code does not make them immune from the insidious, deceptive environment they must constantly negotiate.

Obviously, then, staff welfare, professional supervision and debriefing, along with plenty of down time is essential for any team involved in combating trafficking. Similarly, as I discovered, the importance of working as part of a team and not as a lone ranger cannot be stressed enough. At the very least, two staff should always be deployed to preserve their physical, moral and emotional integrity. This is achieved through open and honest communication, watching each other's back and supporting each other through the dark times.

Security is a major part of any plan to infiltrate a criminal operation. This includes the security of the victims to be rescued. A proper threat assessment should be conducted on every aspect of a proposed mission. This should address everything: where the investigators stay, what cover they will use, which aftercare facilities will be utilized and so on.

In order to ensure that such antitrafficking efforts become self-sustaining, every effort should be made to cultivate, recruit and provide training to local operatives and informants. These indigenous men and women who understand the language, culture and customs of the country in question will ultimately be far more effective in detecting, infiltrating and documenting human trafficking than any foreigner.

Wherever there is the rule of law, however haphazardly and corruptly it is applied, there is an opportunity for a team of professional investigators to present credible and reliable evidence as part of the locally recognized legal process that will be difficult if not impossible to refute. The future of hundreds of thousands of women and children who are currently enslaved rests on the willingness of such people to gather evidence and present it accordingly.

Neither is the fight against modern-day slavery limited to professional investigators. Like the slave trading of previous generations, it requires the combined effort of everyone in our global community to end such pervasive evil. Everyone has a role to play: raising awareness, contributing financial resources, bringing pressure to bear on governments and those responsible for creating and properly enforcing the law, and helping to care for those rescued. This global call to arms is not limited to any country or to any individual, for slaves can be found in the most unlikely places.

One organization more than any other in human history has been charged with seeking justice on behalf of the oppressed and rescuing vulnerable children and advocating for exploited women—the church.

Conclusion

It is curious that physical courage should be so common
in the world and moral courage so rare.

Mother Teresa

I recently executed a search warrant at a home in suburban New
Zealand. The computer was seized and duly examined by the police electronic crime lab. Several hundred images of child abuse
(commonly known as child pornography) were located, and the
suspect was charged accordingly. As I was looking through the
pages and pages of images, my heart froze as I suddenly recognized one of the children. It had only been a few years since I had
carried her terrified little body out of a brothel in Srey Chu, Southeast Asia.

The photograph itself looked strangely familiar. It was then
that I recalled the images taken by the British pedophile. Using
my contacts in the United States, Britain and Southeast Asia, I
arranged for a victim impact statement to be completed on behalf of the child in the photograph. She was still in the care of
Hagar International, an aftercare organization operating in
Southeast Asia. When the offender appeared for sentencing, the
prosecutor was able to transform one photograph among many
into a living, breathing and suffering child. The judge was able

to read firsthand of the impact that the sexual abuse had inflicted on her life.

Dau receives regular counseling, but her counselor reports that she is still reluctant to speak with any real detail about her life in Srey Chu. It is now five years since she was rescued, but she still finds it distressing to talk about. She says she does not want to think about it because every time she thinks of that time she feels sick and has a headache. Dau described her time in Srey Chu as, "a big black hole, and sometimes I am scared I will fall back into it. I don't ever want to think about it again."

Her anxiety levels are still high and she still experiences flashbacks, especially when exposed to triggers of the memories. It may be a motorcycle taxi driving past that reminds her of being taken to meet guests in hotels on the back of a motorcycle or the sight of heavily made-up girls waiting outside a restaurant. Through her artwork Dau has described feeling "broken-hearted and hopeless."

She is a quiet girl with few friends. The counselor reports that Dau says she feels safer being by herself. She has many trust issues. On a scale of 1-10, with 10 indicating the highest level of distress or trauma, Dau rates herself as being a 10 when she was rescued, and is now at 7. She has said, "one day I hope to be a 3, but I know it will never go away."

Below the surface Dau is a hurt little girl, afraid of the memories that still haunt her.

Though possessing and viewing pornography is often seen as a relatively benign or even victimless offense, the sentencing judge deemed it appropriate to make the report public. In doing so he said it was important to remember that every photograph represents a real child with a real name.

RESTORATION

Alice and I are now divorced. There was a time when I did not like the words of Jesus when he said that there would be no marriage in heaven (Matthew 22:30). Now, I find comfort in the knowledge that one day Alice and I will be reconciled, not as a married couple but as fully alive humans in whom there is only perfect love, understanding and acceptance.

I have many unanswered questions. At times the grief has threatened to swallow me alive. But I have discovered that sometimes faith comes down to just choosing to put one foot in front of the other, and that endurance is gained by enduring. Sometimes the greatest miracle is simply holding onto our faith amid the pain and the unanswered prayers, saying stoically and steadfastly like Job, "Though he slay me, yet will I trust him" (Job 13:15 KJV).

As a result of my experiences overseas and all that had occurred, at one point I had pretty much given up on the church. My passion to free those held in slavery remained, and I figured that such victims would have to rely on whatever goodness remained in the world for their rescue and restoration. However, as I have experienced my own inner healing, forgiveness and restoration these last few years, my faith and hope in the church have also been restored.

I have been gently reminded that God loves the broken, fallible and very flawed people who make up the church. The Spirit of God is still at work in and through the church, redeeming people, giving them a second chance and making all things new. And I have embraced the crucified Christ and found faith, hope and love resurrected.

He invites—indeed, commands—us to follow him "into the heart of the dark kingdom, into the soul of what is most evil. He takes us where humankind has chosen to live. He calls us to where the darkness has made those who wander there desperate for light." And as we follow him to those places, he turns us not into heroes but into saints.

NVADER

Imagine what could be achieved if churches around the world began supporting and equipping small teams to infiltrate those brothels where women and children are being held against their will. What if men were applauded and congratulated for using their muscle and risking their lives to protect and defend those weaker than themselves? What would happen within our churches if, in the face of tremendous evil, both men and women used their ingenuity and humble authenticity to effectively and successfully confront it?

What impact would the church then have on our world? What if our evangelism was authentic—instead of trying to manipulate conversations with others, we simply and freely talked about the battle our church was engaged in to free people from all forms of slavery: physical as well as spiritual.

Indeed, what if small teams from every nation began to emerge, were provided training and began sharing information? Using the methods of the criminals against them, what would happen if those with the biblical mandate and freedom to choose to intervene decided to do so?

What is needed is a vehicle through which the church can invade the dark places of human slavery. A team of people who are able to liaise with the church, provide the necessary education, essential training and expertise and then facilitate their engagement with the commercial sexual exploitation of women and children. There are many aspects to ending sex trafficking—and many kinds of work we can take up.

In thinking about developing an organization to focus in investigation and rescue, I wanted a name that symbolized something powerful, proactive and professional. I also wanted a name that would strike fear into the hearts of those who preyed on the innocent and profited from the exploitation of the vulnerable.

I recalled reading a book by Calvin Miller called *The Song*, in which he referred to the Holy Spirit by a name that I thought captured all of these elements. The weird thing was I couldn't recall what the name was. I finally located a copy of the book and found the reference I was looking for:

> The dazzling hurricane of light
> Fell full on [earth's] shame
> And a fiery brilliant radiance
> Proclaimed his mighty name;
> —Invader

"Nvader" is an organization specifically designed to empower small teams from around the world to infiltrate brothels and gather the necessary information to facilitate an intervention resulting in the rescue of victims of human trafficking and the prosecution of those perpetrators responsible (www.nvader.org).

History has shown us what happens when the church acts on behalf of the vulnerable and the oppressed. As far as the forces of evil are concerned, when Christians love with fearless resolve and obey God regardless of the outcome, they are the most dangerous people on earth. "Dark kingdoms tremble; the dungeons and prisons that hold men, women, and children captive crumble; prison doors open; chains unlock; and multitudes come to freedom."

I HAVE A DREAM

On August 28, 1963, at the Lincoln Memorial in Washington, D.C., Martin Luther King Jr. shared his dream. It was a dream based on the belief that God created all men and women equal, that all are entitled to freedom and justice, and that everyone can and should be judged "not by the color of their skin but by the content of their character." His words provoked a response from an otherwise indifferent nation and are credited with mobilizing supporters of desegregation and prompting the enactment of the 1964 Civil Rights Act.

While I do not presume to walk in his shoes, I also believe that God created men and women equal, to follow the same path that leads to freedom and justice for all. And I also have a dream. It is a dream deeply rooted in the freedom and equality I have taken for granted growing up in the small Pacific nation called New Zealand, and while completing my education in the United States.

I have a dream that one day good men and women will rise up and live out the promises they made when their nation's leaders signed global conventions on their behalf, stating that they would take all measures to protect children from all forms of exploitation.

I have a dream that one day in the courtrooms of justice all around the world, former sex slaves will sit across from those who so brutally profited from their shame, and in speaking the truth, find courage, healing and freedom.

I have a dream that one day even the Internet, a medium sizzling with the heat of depravity and the profits of oppression, will be transformed into a sanctuary of hope and an underground of dignified resistance.

I have a dream that the children born into brothels will one day live in a world where they will not be assessed by the ravenous eyes of a predator but will be protected by the strength of courageous men and women who have no greater ambition in life. I have a dream that one day corrupt cops, greedy judges and complicit lawyers will submit to the hard evidence gathered by those simple yet determined individuals working in the struggle to stop the rape-for-profit markets from flourishing further.

I have a dream that small teams of such men and women from all walks of life will use their combined skills and resources to invade the darkest brothels on earth, documenting every abuse and acting on every complaint, persevering until someone, somewhere, intervenes.

I have a dream that churches around the world will come alive with a passion for justice and a hatred of evil, that their goals would no longer be centered around revival or church growth, but the freedom of humanity from all that enslaves and oppresses.

And in doing so, I have a dream that the church would be beautiful—a bride fit for her bridegroom when he returns to establish his kingdom on earth and end all forms of slavery and oppression forever.

Acknowledgments

Words on a page remain lifeless without the breath, touch and loyal friendship of many. However, due to the security concerns associated with this book, I am unable to name most of the people who have made it possible. I hope it is sufficient that you who have made it possible know what you did and that your names are recorded in the book of life.

To my parents, thank you for teaching me to wield the sword of truth, for rescuing me when I needed it and for demonstrating with your lives the power of love.

To my extended family, thanks for your honesty and loving support.

My kiwi mates and American buddies—as iron sharpens iron.

To those gracious friends who helped with the initial reading, thank you for your friendship, encouragement and editorial input.

To all of those who have walked with me in the darkness, both overseas and at home, thank you for the comfort and strength you provided.

My American allies in the field, you have shown by your lives and by your example that it can be done. I am honored to call you friends.

I would perhaps not be alive today without the backup afforded me by many. Thanks for laughing with me and for watching my back.

Thanks to my international support crew, friends and supporters within the New Zealand and American church. I am forever indebted to you all.

I am especially grateful for the wisdom and kind support of both serving and retired New Zealand Police officers.

To my agent and friend Tabitha Plueddemann. You first honored me with your tears, you have encouraged me with your words, and you validated my experience by fighting for the opportunity to share it. Forever and always, thank you.

To Cindy Bunch and her team at IVP Books, thank you for communicating right from the outset that this was more than just another book and that it captured your own heart and imagination as well. I greatly value and cherish your wise guidance and ongoing solidarity.

Last, for security reasons there are a couple of people I cannot mention and do not acknowledge throughout the book. Though your names are not recorded, you are on every page and forever in my heart.

Notes

Chapter 1: South Asia: Her Name Is Daya

p. 17   Sex trafficking is the largest form of modern-day slavery: United Nations Office on Drugs and Crime (UNODC) www .unodc.org/unodc/en/human-trafficking/global-report-on -trafficking-in-persons.html.

p. 17   More than two million children are exploited: United Nations Children's Fund (UNICEF).

Chapter 3: Latin America: Her Name Is Maria

p. 33   "The law has less to do with the reality of the sex industry": Louise Brown, *Sex Slaves* (London: Virago Press, 2000), p. 197.

Chapter 4: Critics

p. 39   Articles 34-35 of the United Nations' "Convention on the Rights of the Child": "Convention on the Rights of the Child," *Office of the High Commissioner for Human Rights*, September 2, 1990, www2.ohchr.org/english/law/crc.htm.

p. 39   "Declaration on the Right and Responsibility of Individuals, Groups and Organs of Society": United Nations General Assembly, March 8, 1999, www.unhchr.ch/huridocda/huridoca .nsf/(symbol)/a.res.53.144.en.

p. 39   "Prevent, Suppress and Punish Trafficking in Persons, Especially Women and Children": United Nations Office of Drugs and Crime, www.unodc.org/unodc/en/human-trafficking/what -is-human-trafficking.html?ref=menuside.

Chapter 5: United States: Her Name Is Jeni

p. 52   "The Internet has facilitated the creation of online communities": Donna Hughes, "Pimps and Predators on the Internet: Globalizing the Sexual Exploitation of Women and Children,"

University of Rhode Island, 1999, www.uri.edu/artsci/wms/
hughes/pprep.htm.

Chapter 6: Dangerous

p. 54   "Life is not a problem to be solved; it is an adventure to be
            lived": John Eldredge, *Wild at Heart* (Nashville: Thomas Nel-
            son, 2001), p. 200.

Chapter 7: Southeast Asia: Her Name Is Mahal

p. 76   Definition of *sex tourism*: ECPAT, www.ecpat.net/ei/Csec_cst
            .asp.

p. 76   Children from poor families become easy targets: UNODC. See
            http://en.wikipedia.org/wiki/Sex_tourism.

p. 76   female children have fewer educational opportunities: UNI-
            CEF. See www.justice.gov/criminal/ceos/sextour.htm.

Chapter 9: Southeast Asia: Their Names Are Lan and Milan

p. 95   The commercial sexual exploitation of children has devastat-
            ing consequences: ECPAT. See www.unicef.org/rosa/commercial
            .pdf.

p. 95   there are over 2 million children enslaved: See www.yapi.org/
            csec.

p. 95   children are more susceptible to HIV and other STDs: See
            http://physiciansforhumanrights.org/library/2003-06-25
            .html.

p. 95   Laws against sexual exploitation of children remain largely un-
            enforced: See www.ecpat.net/worldcongressIII/PDF/Journals/
            EXTRATERRITORIAL_LAWS.pdf.

Chapter 10: Choices

p. 99   "Some of us were in scenes with a lot of hookers": David Fisher,
            "Undercover Officers Risk Deep Damage," *Sunday Star Times*,
            February 8, 2004.

Chapter 11: United States: Her Name Is Emily

p. 112   Organized crime comprises groups or operations run by crimi-
            nals: See www.unodc.org/unodc/en/human-trafficking/index
            .html.

p. 112   billions of dollars made from this criminal activity: See www
            .acf.hhs.gov/trafficking/about/index.html.

p. 112   Organized criminal networks control large parts of the global sex industry: See http://en.wikipedia.org/wiki/Human_trafficking.

p. 112   terrorist groups also make money to further their own political goals: See www.dtic.mil/cgibin/GetTRDoc?Location=U2&doc =GetTRDoc.pdf&AD=ADA448573.

Chapter 12: Undercover

p. 113   "It is the adoption of a false persona": Edwin Delattre, *Character and Cops: Ethics in Policing*, 4th ed. (Lanham, Md.: American Enterprise Institute, 2002), p. 167.

p. 114   "No matter what action is taken, there are moral costs": Ibid., p. 170.

p. 115   law enforcement agencies reassessment of undercover agents: Ibid., p. 171.

p. 115   Undercover work is "more art than science": William Queen, *Under and Alone* (New York: Ballantine, 2006), p. 32.

Chapter 13: Southeast Asia: Their Names Are Phi and Tan

p. 128   Pedophilia is the primary or exclusive sexual attraction: "Pedophilia," *Wikipedia*, http://en.wikipedia.org/wiki/Pedophilia.

p. 128   A large number of pedophiles are respected members of society: Ron O'Grady, *The Rape of the Innocent* (Stockholm: ECPAT, 1992), p. 40.

p. 128   Pedophiles have their own survival manuals and travel guides: Ron O'Grady, *The Child and the Tourist* (Stockholm: ECPAT, 1994), pp. 55-62.

Chapter 14: Church

p. 129   "There may not be a more dangerous weapon for violence": Erwin McManus, *The Barbarian Way* (Nashville: Thomas Nelson, 2005), p. 47.

p. 130   Female infanticide in the first centuries: Rodney Stark, *The Rise of Christianity* (Princeton, N.J.: Princeton University Press, 1996), pp. 97, 118, 124-25. See also Will Durant, *Caesar and Christ* (New York: Simon & Schuster, 1944), pp. 56, 598.

p. 133   "All of us think . . . when we live by faith, we don't die by the sword": McManus, *Barbarian Way*, pp. 38-39.

p. 133   "We've been taught that every story Jesus writes": Ibid., p. 43.

p. 134   "We resist love to avoid pain and squelch our dreams": Ibid., p. 119.

Chapter 15: Southeast Asia: Her Name Is Sua

p. 149   *Facts: HIV/AIDS:* All information is from "Sex Trafficking and
            the HIV/AIDS Pandemic," 2007. Testimony of Holly Burkhalter,
            Physicians for Human Rights, before the U.S. House Interna-
            tional Relations Committee.

Chapter 16: Changes

p. 152   Definition of secondary trauma: Diane Langberg, *Vicarious
            Traumatization: The Cost of Caring* (Philadelphia: Diane Lang-
            berg Ph.D. & Associates, 2004), p. 1.

p. 153   "The center of His will is our only safety": Corrie ten Boom, *The
            Hiding Place* (Grand Rapids: Chosen Books, 1971), p. 84.

Chapter 17: Caribbean: His Name Is Juan

p. 163   Victims of sex trafficking and forced prostitution: Louise
            Brown, *Sex Slaves* (London: Virago Press, 2000), pp. 242, 244.

Chapter 19: Caribbean: Her Name Is Carla

p. 177   "A girl who is raped . . . will frequently be burdened": Louise
            Brown, *Sex Slaves* (London: Virago Press, 2000), p. 39.

p. 177   "A raped girl is unable to marry because she is no longer a vir-
            gin": Ibid.

p. 177   "Prostitution for women is a sin from which": Ibid., p. 238.

p. 177   "The internalization of the bad woman image": Ibid., p. 246.

Chapter 20: Amazing Grace

p. 178   "The love and grace of God is a free gift": John Pritchard, Youth
            For Christ New Zealand. See pp. 21-22.

p. 182   "True strength does not come out of bravado": John Eldredge,
            Wild at Heart (Nashville: Thomas Nelson, 2001), p. 137.

p. 183   "[Our] culture comes along with figures like John Wayne":
            Ibid., p. 122.

p. 186   there is "no pit so deep that [God] is not deeper still": Betsie ten
            Boom, quoted in Corrie ten Boom, *The Hiding Place* (New York:
            Bantam, 1984), p. 217.

p. 187   Definition of *globalization:* "Globalization," *Wikipedia.com,*
            http://en.wikipedia.org/wiki/Globalization.

p. 187   "Virtual enterprises can operate everywhere and nowhere": David
            Batstone, *Not for Sale: The Return of the Global Slave Trade and How
            We Can Fight It* (San Francisco: HarperCollins, 2007), p. 171.

p. 187   "Traffickers, taking advantage of transparent borders": Michele
          A. Clark, "Human Trafficking Casts Shadow on Globalization,"
          YaleGlobal, The Protection Project, Johns Hopkins University
          School of International Studies, 2003.

Conclusion

p. 195   "Dau receives regular counseling but her counselor reports":
          New Zealand Police Victim Impact Report by Daniel Walker
          and Hagar International.

p. 196   "into the heart of the dark kingdom, into the soul of what is
          most evil": Erwin McManus, *The Barbarian Way* (Nashville:
          Thomas Nelson, 2005), p. 134.

p. 198   "The dazzling hurricane of light": Calvin Miller, *The Song*
          (Downers Grove, Ill.: InterVarsity Press, 1977), p. 40.

p. 198   "Dark kingdoms tremble; the dungeons and prisons": Mc-
          Manus, *Barbarian Way*, p. 134.

About NVADER

The methods employed by Nvader are based on best practices and ensure that all of the successes, failures and mistakes outlined in this book, both personal and professional, have been heeded and addressed. Join the invasion at **www.NVADER.org**

To do nothing in the face of evil is to become part of that evil.

author unknown